Communications in Computer and Information Science 1642

More information about this series at https://link.springer.com/bookseries/7899

Carla Rocha · Celio Santana Júnior ·
Fernando De Sá · Tiago Silva da Silva (Eds.)

Agile Methods

11th Brazilian Workshop, WBMA 2021
Virtual Event, October 8–10, 2021
Revised Selected Papers

 Springer

Editors
Carla Rocha ⓘ
Universidade de Brasília
Brasília, Brazil

Celio Santana Júnior ⓘ
Universidade Federal de Pernambuco
Recife, Brazil

Fernando De Sá ⓘ
Instituto Tecnológico de Aeronáutica
São José dos Campos, Brazil

Tiago Silva da Silva ⓘ
Universidade Federal de São Paulo
São José dos Campos, Brazil

ISSN 1865-0929   ISSN 1865-0937 (electronic)
Communications in Computer and Information Science
ISBN 978-3-031-25647-9   ISBN 978-3-031-25648-6 (eBook)
https://doi.org/10.1007/978-3-031-25648-6

Preface

Welcome to the 11th edition of the Brazilian Workshop on Agile Methods (WBMA 2021) held online on October 9, 2021. WBMA is the research track in the Agile Brazil conference. It is an academic event that focuses on agile software development. The workshop has been a reference point for the Brazilian research community in Agile Methods for 11 years, promoting research activities in the field. All the submitted papers – research, experience reports, literature reviews, and position papers – underwent a rigorous peer-review process. At least three members of the Program Committee reviewed each paper. Of the 18 papers submitted, only six were accepted as full papers (33.3%). We also accepted three short papers – experience reports. The Program Committee evaluated each report submission for new experiences that would be both interesting and beneficial to the Brazilian Agile Methods community of academics and practitioners. As usual, we accepted papers dealing with three different aspects of Agile Methods: Agile in education, empirical studies on Agile, and Agile practices. In this edition of WBMA, we had articles addressing topics such as teamwork, software testing, DevOps, User eXperience (UX), software requirements, impacts of COVID-19, and, of course, Scrum. It is worth mentioning that this edition was atypical and quite challenging, considering all the obstacles caused by the global pandemic of COVID-19. We hope the WBMA 2019 proceedings will be helpful for your educational, professional, and academic activities. Finally, we want to thank everyone who contributed to WBMA 2021, including the authors, reviewers, volunteers, and the previous and current chairs. A special thanks to the Agile Brazil conference organizers for their support and partnership.

November 2021

Carla Rocha
Celio Santana Junior
Fernando de Sá
Tiago Silva da Silva

Organization

General Chair

Carla Rocha — Universidade de Brasília, Brazil

Program Committee Chairs

Carla Rocha	Universidade de Brasília, Brazil
Celio Santana Júnior	Universidade Federal de Pernambuco, Brazil
Fernando de Sá	Instituto Tecnológico da Aeronáutica, Brazil
Tiago Silva da Silva	Universidade Federal de São Paulo, Brazil

Steering Committee

Alfredo Goldman	Universidade de São Paulo, Brazil
Carla Rocha	Universidade de Brasília, Brazil
Celio Santana Júnior	Universidade Federal de Pernambuco, Brazil
Eduardo Guerra	Free University of Bolzen-Bolzano, Italy
Paulo Meirelles	Universidade Federal do ABC, Brazil
Rafael Prikladnicki	Pontifícia Universidade Católica do Rio Grande do Sul, Brazil
Tiago Silva da Silva	Universidade Federal de São Paulo, Brazil

Program Committee

Ademar Aguiar	Universidade do Porto, Portugal
Elder Cirilo	Universidade Federal de São João del-Rei, Brazil
Filipe Correia	Universidade do Porto, Portugal
Heitor Costa	Universidad Federal de Lavras, Brazil
Fernando de Sá	Instituto Tecnológico da Aeronáutica, Brazil
Eduardo Figueiredo	Universidade Federal de Minas Gerais, Brazil
Felipe Furtado	CESAR School, Brazil
Alejandra Garrido	Universidad Nacional de La Plata, Argentina
Alfredo Goldman	Universidade de São Paulo, Brazil
Eduardo Guerra	Free University of Bolzen-Bolzano, Italy
Celio Santana Júnior	Universidade Federal de Pernambuco, Brazil
Fabio Kon	Universidade de São Paulo, Brazil
Fábio Levy Siqueira	Universidade de São Paulo, Brazil

Contents

x   Contents

Full Papers

Using a Teamwork Quality Instrument to Improve Agile Teams' Effectiveness: Practical Use Cases

Arthur Freire[✉], Manuel Neto, Mirko Perkusich[✉], Alexandre Costa,
Kyller Gorgônio, Hyggo Almeida, and Angelo Perkusich

Intelligent Software Engineering (ISE) Group @ VIRTUS,
Federal University of Campina Grande, Campina Grande, Brazil
{arthurfreire,manuel}@copin.ufcg.edu.br,
{mirko,alexandre.costa,kyller,hyggo,perkusic}@virtus.ufcg.edu.br

Abstract. Agile Software Development (ASD) has become the most chosen development method. The core fundamentals of ASD are based on Teamwork factors and how valuable it considers individuals and their interactions over processes and tools. Researchers have shown the positive impact of teamwork quality in ASD and the importance of assessing it to increase the chances of succeeding projects in this context. Based on this, some researchers have proposed instruments that can assess ASD teamwork quality. One of these instruments is a bayesian network-based model (TWQ-BN), with its practical utility assessed in a case study presented in previous work. However, there is a lack of practical use cases documented using TWQ-BN to identify process improvement opportunities. This paper addresses this gap by presenting two industry-based use cases to help potential users understand how to use TWQ-BN to define action items to improve the team's effectiveness. This paper provides better guidance toward adopting TWQ-BN and shows how it can be used as a tool on iteration retrospectives to diagnose the teamwork quality.

Keywords: Teamwork · Agile Software Development · Bayesian networks · Use cases

1 Introduction

Agile Software Development (ASD) is a lightweight approach for developing software when compared with traditional plan-driven approaches. Usually, agile initiatives embrace iterative development, which can be translated into dividing the delivery process into short iterations, allowing requirements to be refined on a regular basis [10]. According to Hoda et al. [12], ASD has become the mainstream development method of choice.

ASD is oriented by the principles described in the Agile Manifesto [3], which states that ASD values individuals and the interactions between them more than processes and tools [11]. The Agile Manifesto evidences the team's importance by having six out of twelve principles directly related to the team (i.e., individuals).

© Springer Nature Switzerland AG 2023
C. Rocha et al. (Eds.): WBMA 2021, CCIS 1642, pp. 3–17, 2023.
https://doi.org/10.1007/978-3-031-25648-6_1

Studies have shown the positive impact of teamwork quality (TWQ) [13,14], and its relevance for success in ASD [4,8,20,22,23]. Batista et al. [2] discussed that the effective combination of individual parts, often carried out by software development teams, requires interactions among team members and the coordination of interdependent individual and team level tasks. Given its impact, researchers argued about the importance of assessing teamwork quality to increase the chances of succeeding with ASD [2,9].

Moreover, some researchers have proposed instruments for assessing ASD teamwork quality. Moe et al. [21] presented a Radar Plot that considers five dimensions: *Shared Leadership, Team Orientation, Redundancy, Learning,* and *Autonomy.* Lindsjørn et al. [16] presented a Structural Equation Model, based on a differentiated replication [15] from a study by Hoegl and Gemuenden [13], which considered that the teamwork construct is comprised of six variables: *Communication, Coordination, Balance of Member Contribution, Mutual Support, Effort,* and *Cohesion.* Finally, Freire et al. [9] proposed a Bayesian networks-based model with 16 variables, which had its practical utility positively assessed in a case study.

Moe et al. [21] present two cases of using their proposed model for diagnosing the teamwork quality and supporting the teams to improve their processes. Conversely, the instrument presented by Lindsjørn et al. [16] is based on Structural Equation Modeling, which is not suited for supporting decision-making [1]. In Freire et al. [9], the researchers stated that subjects involved in the case study applying their instrument reported that "the model outputs are useful on detecting weaknesses and strengths to allow continuous improvement of the teamwork quality". However, the paper does not detail how the teams used the instrument to identify action items. Therefore, despite the instrument presented by Freire et al. [9] be promising, its adoption is not supported by practical use cases, which are vital for the industry to adopt any data-driven initiative [7].

This paper addresses this gap by presenting two industry-based use cases that demonstrate how practitioners can use the instrument proposed by Freire et al. [9] to assess and improve ASD teamwork quality continuously, and to increase the team's effectiveness. We defined these use cases based on the first author's previous experiences during the COVID-19 pandemic while working on a scaled agile environment within a Fortune 50 company. The use cases presented in this paper aim to motivate the adoption of the instrument [9] by providing better guidance for practitioners towards its usage in the industry.

The remaining of this paper is organized as follows. Section 2 describes the teamwork quality instruments presented by Moe et al. [21] and Freire et al. [9], as well as information about software development teams working from home during COVID-19 pandemic. Section 3 presents this study's methodology. Section 4 presents two use cases for the teamwork quality instrument presented by Freire et al. [9]. Section 5 discusses this study's main findings and implications. Finally, Sect. 6 presents our final remarks and future work.

2   Background and Related Works

2.1   Team Radar Plot Usage to Diagnose and Improve Teamwork

Ringstad et al. [22] applied the Team Radar plot, proposed by Moe et al. [21], in two teams from different companies to diagnose teamwork towards its improvement. According to the authors, the diagnosis phase consisted of collecting data through observation and semi-structured interviews. The first author was responsible for observing teamwork practice in daily work and ceremonies like daily meetings, iteration planning, and retrospective. The teamwork diagnosis final results were scores on a scale [0, 10] (inclusive) on selected team radar factors. The scores were based on the collected answers from all team members and the observed practice notes. The diagnosis for both teams is presented in Fig. 1.

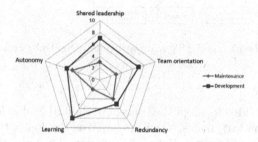

Fig. 1. The radar plot of teamwork characteristics of the *maintenance and development teams*, from [22].

Ringstad et al. [22] stated that the action planning intended to specify organizational actions that should either relieve the primary problems identified in the diagnosis or improve them. Besides, they also state that, in action research, a theoretical framework (i.e., Team Radar) should guide the diagnosis phases' plan. They organized the diagnosis phases' results into a presentation alongside the problems and consequences to the teams, and let their members openly discuss whether they recognized how teamwork should be presented in the results. Then, they discussed which areas should receive priority to improve teamwork, and, finally, discussed concreted actions to build up an action plan.

2.2   Teamwork Bayesian Network Model (TWQ-BN)

Freire et al. [9] present a Bayesian networks-based model (hereafter addressed by TWQ-BN) to assess and improve the teamwork quality in the ASD context. Further, they detail a procedure to apply the proposed model.

To build the model, the authors listed many ASD teamwork key factors extracted from the literature. Based on the knowledge of an expert and the resulting list, they used reasoning on a top-down approach - starting with the target factor (i.e., teamwork quality) - breaking down higher-level factors into others they judged more observable. Figure 2. presents the directed acyclic graph (DAG) representing the final version of TWQ-BN factors and their relationships. In this DAG, we define the nodes with arrows coming out from them to other(s) as parent nodes, and consequently, the ones with arrows coming in are defined as child nodes.

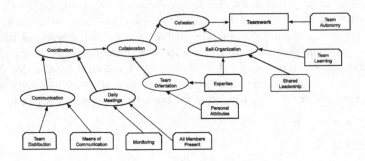

Fig. 2. Bayesian network based ASD teamwork quality model by Freire et al. [9] (TWQ-BN)

The authors decided to adopt the concept of Ranked Nodes [5] to represent all dependent (i.e., non-leaf) nodes, which are based on the double truncated Normal distribution (TNormal) limited in the [0, 1] region. They also defined that each node comprises a 5-point Likert scale (i.g., *Very Low, Low, Medium, High,* and *Very High*). To build the nodes' probability tables, the authors established a set of questions for the expert, who replied with a probability for each child node's state based on the combination of each parent node's state.

Freire et al. evaluated TWQ-BN's practical utility in a case study conducted with three units of analysis (i.e., ASD teams) that used *Scrum*. There were three subjects involved in the case study, being the *Scrum Masters* of the teams. TWQ-BN was applied during forty-five days (i.e., three sprints).

After executing the case study, the authors concluded that TWQ-BN model assists agile teams on assessing teamwork quality and identifying improvement opportunities, is easy to learn, and the cost-benefit for using it with the proposed procedure is positive. However, in this case study the researchers did not focus on the action items that resulted from the analysis of the outputs of TWQ-BN after each sprint.

2.3 Software Development Teams Working from Home During COVID-19

Miller et al. [19] ran an exploratory survey during the early months of the COVID-19 pandemic with 2265 developer responses. The results revealed that many developers faced challenges reaching milestones and that their team productivity had changed. The authors also found through qualitative analysis that important team culture factors such as communication and social connection had been affected. According to their results, the ability to brainstorm with colleagues, difficulty communicating with colleagues, and satisfaction with interactions from social activities are important factors that are associated with how developers report their software development team's productivity.

Mendonça et al. [18] presented their experience in managing the expectations and changing the development methods to mitigate the risks of carrying out a research and development project during a pandemic time. According to them, even though the development team quickly adapted itself to working from home, there were some impact on the development plans. The authors stated that trying to reconcile the trade-offs between completeness and the tight schedule for the first release was a challenge, given that they depended on different partners to collect the information they need to make available in a mobile application that corresponds to one of the outcomes.

3   Methodology

The definition of the use cases was done considering the specific context of an ASD team during the COVID-19 pandemic. This section presents the process that we adopted to define practical, real-world-based use cases, aiming to demonstrate how practitioners can use TWQ-BN to assess and improve ASD teamwork quality continuously.

Next, Sect. 3.1 details the context which inspired defining the use cases presented herein. Further, Sect. 3.2 discusses how we adapted TWQ-BN to suit the context of our research better, and, finally, Sect. 3.3 presents the process that we employed to define the uses cases.

3.1   Research Context

We defined the use cases based on the first author's experiences during the COVID-19 pandemic while working from home. The team on which the use cases were based comprises one software development manager, one quality assurance engineer, seven software development engineers, and one software development engineer intern.

This team was part of a Fortune 50 multinational company working on a big project that required the development of new components and extensions on existing ones to provide a set of features for its customers, making sure to comply with tax and compliance regulations. This project was developed in a scaled agile environment, comprising many software teams.

The team's work addressed in this paper was focused on the implementation of three new microservices and extending existing ones' capabilities, which will be hereafter addressed as workstreams. The technology stack and business context of each of the four main workstreams were very distinct. Also, some business requirements required interaction between the components of the four workstreams, and components owned and developed by other teams.

The software development engineers and the intern divided themselves into two people working on each workstream. They divided the workload across them to ensure the team would be able to deliver their assigned work.

The team used Scrumban, which means that they relied on managing tasks with a Kanban board, limited work-in-progress (WIP), and analyzed their workflow through lead and cycle time analysis. Moreover, the team adopted one-month iterations and pushed work given the requirements' estimates (i.e., Story Points) and using its velocity. The ASD ceremonies adopted by the team were daily meetings and iteration retrospectives. Even though Kanban does not prescribe planning User Stories and tasks - because work is planned based on the number of cards and the average lead and cycle time of previous ones - this team used to estimate the User Stories considered "ready" (i.e., defined and agreed acceptance criteria) by doing ad-hoc plannings.

The project's design and development phases only started after the scoping and definition of the high-level requirements. These high-level requirements were translated into Epics placed into the Project Backlog. This backlog was shared by all teams involved in the project, and depending on an Epic's abstractness, the ownership for delivering it could be split by more than one team. For each Epic in the backlog, either the business stakeholders would assign them to the correct team based on their knowledge, or the teams themselves would take ownership based on the Epic's similarities with the teams' current responsibilities.

The refinement of these requirements occurred continuously while design and development phases were occurring. The translation of Epics (i.e., high-level requirements) into tasks was incremental and depended on the design and development phases. For each Epic owned by the team addressed in this paper, it was necessary to work on the architectural designs of new or existing components. These designs usually involved people from other teams to define interfaces and responsibilities between their components and approvals whenever needed (e.g., one team making changes to an existing platform owned by another team to support a new use case). The designs were addressed as User Stories under the Epic, and their definitions were considered deliverables artifacts because the created documentation helped maintain the company stack up to date.

These designs helped refine the Epics and on defining User Stories that considered development work. Based on the tasks necessary to complete the User Stories, the team members ran ad-hoc plannings to estimate them using Story Points. These estimates also served as the basis for requirements refinement because the effort could extrapolate the project plan and compromise the deadline.

At the end of each month, the team executed iteration retrospectives to identify the things that went well and the bad ones. For the bad things, the team used to define action items, a deadline, and an owner responsible for engaging the necessary people to avoid those bad things from happening again. Since the team did not own a product and there was no incremental delivery, there was no iteration review. However, the team velocity assessment was done by the team manager, with the purpose of reporting and raising possible related risks that could compromise the project deadline.

3.2 TWQ-BN Adaptation

We adapted TWQ-BN to suit the context described in Sect. 3.1, which included a team working fully remote and using Scrumban. Figure 3 presents the adapted version of TWQ-BN and marks with a red-colored "X" the nodes that we removed from the original BN.

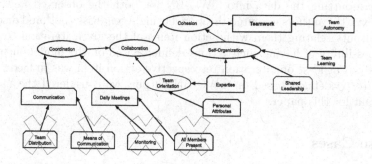

Fig. 3. TWQ-BN adaptation for use cases definition (Color figure online)

Given that the team worked fully remotely, we removed the nodes *Team Distribution* and *Means of Communication*, because they were originally tuned as if that team had to be co-located for having a "good" communication. Thus, we considered *Communication* as a leaf node.

We also removed the nodes *Monitoring* and *All Members Present*, which were originally parents of the *Daily Meetings* node, turning *Daily Meetings* into a leaf node. This means that both *Monitoring* and *All Members Present* were removed. This decision is based on the dynamics and maturity of the team, that did not require all members to be present, and had good documentation mechanisms on the tasks to keep the ongoing statuses up to date.

3.3 Use Cases Definition Process

We defined the use cases for using TWQ-BN to improve agile teams' effectiveness by following the steps presented in what follows.

1. The first author reviewed iteration retrospective meetings' notes and specific retrospective cards used on an online retrospective board tool, restricted to internal usage by the company's employees only;
2. For each iteration retrospective, the first author retrieved the action items defined, remembered the team's environment context at that time and the problems that resulted on their definition;

3. For each set comprising one iteration retrospective, action items, and their causes, the first author defined the environmental context in which the team was inserted by writing a few paragraphs. This set of information (i.e., iteration retrospective environmental context, the action items defined on this ceremony, and their causes) defines the structure for the defined use cases;
4. The authors discussed each use case separately. During the discussions, the first author was asked to input data to TWQ-BN based on his memories of the team context at the time (i.e., observed context). Also, the first author was asked to input data into the model based on the expectations of what the team wanted to achieve as a result of the action items (i.e., target context);
5. After inputting the data into TWQ-BN for both the observed and target contexts, the authors executed the model using AgenaRisk tool[1] and discussed its outputs relating them with action items of the given iteration to assess the possibility of having such actions defined based on the model output.
6. Finally, if at least one iteration retrospective action item was judged as possible to be defined based on TWQ-BN output, we considered the use case relevant for this paper.

4   Use Cases

This section presents two use cases that are based on the first author's industry experience. The first use case addresses problems on team *Communication, Daily Meetings, Redundancy,* and *Team Learning.* The second use case focuses on problems on *Team Autonomy* and *Team Learning.* Notice that such use cases conform with the scope of iteration retrospective events, in which the team reflects on how to be more effective. Due to the lack of space, Use Case #2 won't have the images.

For both use cases, we describe the context (i.e., Context Description) and explain how TWQ-BN should be fed given it (i.e., Data Input). Further, we discuss how the team could use TWQ-BN to support its decision-making process for identifying improvement opportunities and action items to be executed (i.e., Analysis). In what follows, we describe both use cases.

4.1   Use Case #1

Context Description. As mentioned in Sect. 3.1, the team subdivided into pairs to work on separate workstreams, which contained inter-dependencies. As a consequence, during the daily meetings, while the owner of a given card related to a specific workstream explained his/her tasks' current status, the other team members working on different workstreams could not understand some of the details or got curious to understand better the work done by the teammate. Moreover, sometimes, members that were working on a specific workstream initiated very detailed discussions. These situations resulted in longer daily meetings because of the additional discussions attempting to explain each workstream's

---

[1] https://agenarisk.com.

specifics to the members not working on it. Besides, as this happened at the beginning of the work-from-home phase, many ad-hoc remote meetings were scheduled, attempting to get the team members on the same page regarding the specific details. However, the team members' new routines made it difficult to accommodate everyone in the same time slot. This occurred because they were not yet used to the many remote meetings instead of casual conversations that used to occur while working in the office.

Data Input. Based on the problems related to the daily meetings losing focus and the communication issues, we inputted the values *Low* into the leaf nodes *Communication* and *Daily Meetings*. Further, the team members only had a high-level, insufficient understanding of the workstreams they did not work with, mainly because the team's mechanics to exchange such knowledge was inefficient. Given this, we inputted the values *Low* and *Medium* into the leaf nodes *Expertise* and *Team Learning*, respectively. We inputted data into the node *Expertise* because it considers the team's redundancy in its definition, and at that point, the team had knowledge silos. The remaining leaf nodes were left without inputs because they were not relevant for this use case, and Bayesian networks can handle the absence of data.

Figure 4 presents the outputs calculated by TWQ-BN given the inputs previously explained. In Fig. 4, notice that the leaf nodes that we inputted data are marked with a rectangle. For instance, the leaf node *Daily Meeting* is marked with an orange rectangle with the information "Observed: Low", meaning that we inputted the value *Low* into this node for this use case. Further, notice that the leaf nodes' descendants are represented with a box, which includes a bar graph. The bar graph represents the probability that the given variable has for the possible states/value. For instance, the node *Collaboration* has a calculated probability of 21.747% of being *Very Low*, 72.408% of being *Low*, and 5.829% of being *Medium*.

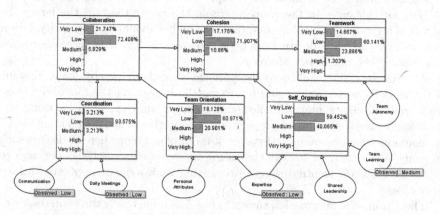

Fig. 4. TWQ-BN inputs and calculated outputs for use case #1 (Color figure online)

Analysis. By analyzing the TWQ-BN's calculated values (see Fig. 4), users can diagnose their team's teamwork quality, which is an indicator of its effectiveness. For this purpose, the users do not need to worry about the specific probabilities but only about the central tendency. For instance, for analyzing the bar graph for *Teamwork*, the users can interpret that their team's overall teamwork quality is highly likely to be "low" (i.e., "bad"), which might affect its performance and delivered product's quality (i.e., prognosis).

Given the calculated values, the team could have a broader goal, focusing on improving the overall teamwork quality (i.e., the *Teamwork* node) or a more specific one, focusing on one of the intermediate nodes. For instance, given this use case's description, the team primarily focused on its *Cohesion*, and not much about its overall *Teamwork* quality. Notice that this observation follows from the leaf nodes in which data were inputted, and *Autonomy*, the other parent of *Teamwork* had no input data. Further, alternatively, in practice, the order of decisions could be the inverse. First, select one or more intermediate target nodes to focus on. Then, select which leaf nodes to collect data for.

At this point, the team would have diagnosed its teamwork quality and would identify improvement opportunities. The improvement opportunities follow from the leaf nodes that the team inputted data to and that could improve. In this case, the team could improve *Daily Scrum, Communication, Team Learning*, and *Expertise*. Notice that there might have more improvement opportunities for the remaining leaf nodes, but it could be out of the scope of the team's current concerns, which we are assuming to be the case here.

The team's next step is to prioritize the improvement opportunities. Bayesian networks nodes can depend on the values of many other nodes, directly or indirectly. For this purpose, it's possible to run a sensitivity analysis to analyze which of the analyzed leaf nodes have a more significant impact on *Cohesion*. Sensitivity analysis provides means to understand the nodes that have the highest impact on a target node.

Figure 5 shows the tornado graph representing the results of the sensitivity analysis for this case. In the tornado graph, the larger the bar, the larger the impact of a given node in *Cohesion*; thus, the higher should be its priority. Given this, we have that the priority, from higher to lower, is *Expertise, Team Learning, Communication*, and *Daily Meetings*.

Alternatively, the team could also perform what-if analysis by changing some of the model's nodes' values and observing the impact on the remaining ones. Such analysis allows more detailed and complex analysis, such as using the Bayesian Network's backward propagation capabilities, called "explaining away" or "nonmonotonic reasoning". However, it is out of our scope here to discuss such an analysis. Further, we believe that using the sensitivity analysis is enough to guide the team on identifying and prioritizing improvement opportunities for most cases.

Then, using the information shown in Fig. 5 as a reference, the team discusses action items. Since, from the candidate nodes, *Expertise* is the one with the most significant impact on *Cohesion* (that is, the team's target), the team could first come up with candidate action items to improve it. For this factor, an action

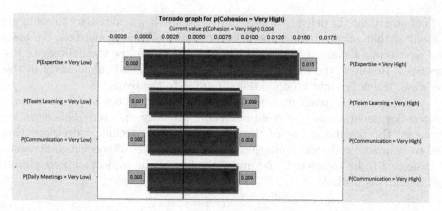

Fig. 5. Sensitivity analysis for *Cohesion*, considering the value *Very High* (exported from AgenaRisk tool)

item could be to have recurrent weekly meetings in which the team members of each workstream handled by the team would be responsible for explaining the technical details and trade-offs being faced by them, in an informal format that allows the others to ask questions openly and discuss. Notice that this action item takes part of the team's capacity and affects the factor *Team Learning* and *Communication*.

The next improvement opportunity to be analyzed is *Daily Scrum*. For this factor, an action item could be to have one person responsible for coaching and keeping the ceremony within its focus. Notice that this action item requires minimum effort.

At the end of this process, the team would have a set of candidate action items to execute. As with any decision, to decide which action items to execute, the team should consider, at least, their value (i.e., impact) and required effort. However, other context-sensitive factors could also be considered.

4.2   Use Case #2

Context Description. During an iteration, a new high-priority requirement (i.e., Epic) emerged to address gaps that were not identified during the scoping phase. These gaps were not previously addressed because the Business team made assumptions without consulting other stakeholders with the required knowledge.

The project involved many teams working in parallel to address different requirements, and this new Epic did not have an owner when it was placed in the Project Backlog. However, upper management decided that the team addressed in this paper should deliver it without removing any of the already planned User Stories. To accommodate this new Epic, they needed to sacrifice quality, which increased the team's technical debt backlog.

Moreover, one of the team's services relied on the functioning of a service owned by another team to deliver critical messages. However, this other service did not guarantee the delivery of such messages, and it was necessary to configure a monitor that alarmed when the deliveries failed. When it alarmed, the team had to execute a manual, error-prone process to guarantee the delivery of lost messages. However, the number of lost messages increased significantly in this iteration, which brought an operational burden to the team.

Additionally, the team members were complaining about the workstreams-related documentations that were not being properly updated. This situation impacted the understanding of the reasons for some technical decisions that had to be made, technical limitations or responsibilities of specific components that needed to be connected, and understanding of the project's bigger picture architecture as a whole.

Data Input. Based on the problems that followed from the team's obligation to handle the new Epic, and the increase in team's operational burden, we inputted the value *Low* into the leaf node *Autonomy*. This decision is based on the team members' feeling of not having control over their boundaries and their incapability to tackle a problem impacting their day-to-day routines without the other team's engagement.

Further, we reflected the issue of the team not documenting, and not having general understanding of project as a whole, as the value *Medium* into the leaf node *Team Learning*. As with the Use Case #1, we left the remaining leaf nodes without inputs.

The outputs calculated by TWQ-BN based on the previous inputs resulted on the following probabilities for the *Teamwork* node: 15.274% of being *Very Low*, 48.05% of being *Low*, 31.524% of being *Medium*, and 5.02% of being *High*.

Analysis. The probabilities calculated by TWQ-BN for the *Teamwork* node are more concentrated in *Low*, but also with a considerable tendency to *Medium*. There's only one common non-leaf node that both *Team Learning* and *Autonomy* impact: *Teamwork*. Therefore, the team's focus in this use case would be this node.

The sensitivity analysis for *Teamwork* node based on the leaf nodes considered in this use case calculated that *Autonomy* has a higher impact on *Teamwork* than *Team Learning*, having a higher priority.

In this case, action items could be (i) an engagement with business to require consultation of stakeholders before making assumptions, which would have avoided the definition of the new priority Epic on short-notice; and (ii) a formal engagement, with escalations if needed, with the team owning the messages delivery service to define a long-term solution to avoid the issues, but with an initial improvement that could reduce manual operational burden. These action items would directly impact *Autonomy*. If they were implemented and caused a positive impact (i.e., *Autonomy* value as *Very High*), the overall value of *Teamwork* would switch to *Medium* (i.e., 43.67%), with a small chance of being *High* (i.e., 17.03%), which indicates how important it is to respect the team's autonomy.

For *Team Learning*, the action item could be to consider User Stories and their tasks "done", only when the related documentation was up to date, reflecting the changes addressed by their contexts. The task reviewers would be responsible for verifying if such updates were in place prior to approving the work done in a given task.

5   Discussion

We defined both use cases (see Sect. 4) based on the industry experience of this paper's first author. As mentioned previously, they were based on the context of a team using Scrumban. One might argue that the team was not following agile "by the book", but such deviations are frequent in industry [17].

The use cases demonstrated how TWQ-BN could help agile teams to decide which TWQ dimensions needed improvement by informing them about which factors should be analyzed (i.e., the BN's nodes). This characteristic can be compared to a checklist, which is a widely used mechanism to support decision-making. Further, the team can analyze TWQ-BN to prioritize action items by running a sensitivity analysis or "what-if" scenarios. Notice that an action item can impact multiple factors, and multiple action item can impact a single factor. It is up to the team, after analyzing TWQ-BN, to decide which action item to implement.

We believe that the fact that TWQ-BN is based on BN is an advantage to support decision-making when compared to other TWQ instruments such as the ones presented by Moe et al. [20] and Lindsjørn et al. [16]. Comparing to Moe et al. [20], both can be used to diagnose TWQ, but TWQ-BN has the advantage of computing the impact of each factor on the overall TWQ and gives the team the flexibility to perform "what-if" scenarios to support their decisions. This characteristic follows from being possible to model richer information in a Bayesian Network than with a radar plot, which includes handling missing data, explicit capturing of each unknown variable, no fixed list of input and output variables, which enables diagnosis and prognosis, and easier understanding of the relationships between variables [6]. Regarding Lindsjørn et al. [16], a clear disadvantage is that it is based on Structural Equation Modeling, which is known not to be suitable for supporting decision-making [1].

Agile teams frequently reflect on how to be more effective, usually during iteration retrospective events. TWQ-BN could be used to support such events. Thus, practitioners could refer to the use cases presented herein as references for adopting TWQ-BN for improving their teams.

However, as pointed by Figalist et al. [7], having use cases is not enough to encourage practitioners to adopt artificial intelligence or software analytics. It is also necessary to have, for instance, the necessary infrastructure (i.e., tool). A limitation of TWQ-BN is because the model currently only runs on a Bayesian Network-specific tool, requiring users to entering data directly into the tool. Thus, future research lines could ease the effort of inputting data into the model and for practitioners to interpret the findings. Further, it would be helpful if

TWQ-BN could provide ideas of action items for practitioners, especially for less mature teams.

6   Conclusions

This paper presented two industry-based use cases demonstrating how agile teams can use TWQ-BN [9] to identify action items and improve their effectiveness. Thus, agile teams can use it as a reference to adopting it.

A study's limitation is that it does not cover more advanced analysis, including "explaining away", which can help agile teams to define action items. Further, TWQ-BN does not claim external validity; thus, it might be possible for the team to need to adapt it to fit its context, which might include modifying its graph, probability functions, and data sources (i.e., data used to input data into the model's nodes). Thus, in future work, we will develop guidelines on how to make such adaptations.

A known limitation of TWQ-BN is its dependency on AgenaRisk, which hinders its adoption due to its limitation to integrate with agile teams' tools. Thus, in future work, we will develop the required infrastructure to ease its adoption by practitioners.

Finally, an open question is for which team profile would TWQ-BN be more helpful. One could argue that mature teams could figure out how to improve without the need for such a tool, with no harm. Further, it could be more beneficial for less mature teams. In any case, it could be more valuable if it provided ideas for action items. We also plan to explore this question in future works.

References

1. Anderson, R.D., Vastag, G.: Causal modeling alternatives in operations research: overview and application. Eur. J. Oper. Res. **156**(1), 92–109 (2004)
2. Batista, A.C.D., de Souza, R.M., da Silva, F.Q.B., de Almeida Melo, L., Marsicano, G.: Teamwork quality and team success in software development: a non-exact replication study. In: Proceedings of the 14th ACM/IEEE International Symposium on Empirical Software Engineering and Measurement (ESEM), ESEM 2020. Association for Computing Machinery, New York (2020)
3. Beck, K., et al.: Manifesto for agile software development (2001). http://www.agilemanifesto.org/
4. Chow, T., Cao, D.B.: A survey study of critical success factors in agile software projects. J. Syst. Softw. **81**(6), 961–971 (2008)
5. Fenton, N., Neil, M., Caballero, J.G.: Using ranked nodes to model qualitative judgments in Bayesian networks. IEEE Trans. Knowl. Data Eng. **19**(10), 1420–1432 (2007)
6. Fenton, N., Neil, M., Marsh, W., Hearty, P., Radliński, L, Krause, P.: On the effectiveness of early life cycle defect prediction with Bayesian nets. Empirical Softw. Eng. **13**(5), 499–537 (2008). https://doi.org/10.1007/s10664-008-9072-x
7. Figalist, I., Elsner, C., Bosch, J., Olsson, H.H.: Breaking the vicious circle: why AI for software analytics and business intelligence does not take off in practice. In: 2020 46th Euromicro Conference on Software Engineering and Advanced Applications (SEAA), pp. 5–12. IEEE (2020)

8. Fontana, R.M., Fontana, I.M., da Rosa Garbuio, P.A., Reinehr, S., Malucelli, A.: Processes versus people: how should agile software development maturity be defined? J. Syst. Softw. **97**, 140–155 (2014)
9. Freire, A., Perkusich, M., Saraiva, R., Almeida, H., Perkusich, A.: A Bayesian networks-based approach to assess and improve the teamwork quality of agile teams. Inf. Softw. Technol. **100**, 119–132 (2018)
10. Gren, L., Goldman, A., Jacobsson, C.: Agile ways of working: a team maturity perspective. J. Softw. Evol. Process **32**(6), e2244 (2020)
11. Gren, L., Lenberg, P.: Agility is responsiveness to change: an essential definition. In: Proceedings of the Evaluation and Assessment in Software Engineering, pp. 348–353. Association for Computing Machinery (2020)
12. Hoda, R., Salleh, N., Grundy, J.: The rise and evolution of agile software development. IEEE Softw. **35**(5), 58–63 (2018)
13. Hoegl, M., Gemuenden, H.G.: Teamwork quality and the success of innovative projects: a theoretical concept and empirical evidence. Organ. Sci. **12**(4), 435–449 (2001)
14. Kraut, R.E., Streeter, L.A.: Coordination in software development. Commun. ACM **38**(3), 69–81 (1995)
15. Lindsay, R.M., Ehrenberg, A.S.C.: The design of replicated studies. Am. Stat. **47**(3), 217–228 (1993)
16. Lindsjørn, Y., Sjøberg, D.I., Dingsøyr, T., Bergersen, G.R., Dybå, T.: Teamwork quality and project success in software development: a survey of agile development teams. J. Syst. Softw. **122**, 274–286 (2016)
17. Masood, Z., Hoda, R., Blincoe, K.: Real world scrum a grounded theory of variations in practice. IEEE Trans. Softw. Eng. **48**(5), 1579–1591 (2022)
18. de Mendonça, W.L.M., et al.: From dusk till dawn: reflections on the impact of COVID-19 on the development practices of a R&D project. In: Proceedings of the 34th Brazilian Symposium on Software Engineering, SBES 2020, pp. 596–605. Association for Computing Machinery, New York (2020). https://doi.org/10.1145/3422392.3422446
19. Miller, C., Rodeghero, P., Storey, M.A., Ford, D., Zimmermann, T.: "How was your weekend?" Software development teams working from home during COVID-19. In: 2021 IEEE/ACM 43rd International Conference on Software Engineering (ICSE), pp. 624–636 (2021)
20. Moe, N.B., Dingsøyr, T., Dybå, T.: A teamwork model for understanding an agile team: a case study of a scrum project. Inf. Softw. Technol. **52**(5), 480–491 (2010)
21. Moe, N.B., Dingsøyr, T., Røyrvik, E.A.: Putting agile teamwork to the test – an preliminary instrument for empirically assessing and improving agile software development. In: Abrahamsson, P., Marchesi, M., Maurer, F. (eds.) XP 2009. LNBIP, vol. 31, pp. 114–123. Springer, Heidelberg (2009). https://doi.org/10.1007/978-3-642-01853-4_14
22. Ringstad, M.A., Dingsøyr, T., Brede Moe, N.: Agile process improvement: diagnosis and planning to improve teamwork. In: O'Connor, R.V., Pries-Heje, J., Messnarz, R. (eds.) EuroSPI 2011. CCIS, vol. 172, pp. 167–178. Springer, Heidelberg (2011). https://doi.org/10.1007/978-3-642-22206-1_15
23. Williams, L., Rubin, K., Cohn, M.: Driving process improvement via comparative agility assessment. In: Proceedings of the 2010 Agile Conference, AGILE 2010, Washington, DC, USA, pp. 3–10. IEEE Computer Society (2010)

Agile Methodology Brazilian Workshop - Agile Brazil: A Decade of Software Testing

Acássio dos A. Araújo[1], Jhonatan S. de Castro[1], Ana Melo[1,2],
Rodrigo B. Cursino[1], and Wylliams B. Santos[1,2(✉)]

[1] CESAR School, Recife, Pernambuco, Brazil
{aaa,jsc,rbc}@cesar.school, accm@ecomp.poli
[2] University of Pernambuco, Recife, Pernambuco, Brazil
wbs@upe.br

Abstract. Due to concerns with agile testing scenario in Brazil, this paper presents the mapping (2010–2019) and analysis of the research on software testing published on Agile Methodology Brazilian Workshop (WBMA), Agile Brazil throughout these years. Such work aims to verify the development, the diversity of papers related to software testing and arising from the concerns with the studies of the testing scenario in agile methods in Brazil; this paper presents the mapping (2010–2019) and analysis on the development of research in software testing in papers published in the Brazilian Workshop on Agile Methods (WBMA), Agile Brazil. The paper used systematic literature review practices, enabling qualitative and quantitative analysis of the collected evidence. This effort aims to verify the growth, the diversity of approaches linked to the use of testing in the broader context of agile methodologies and to make notes on the profile of the papers, given the strengthening of studies in the area in the last decade, in spaces of academic discussion and applications in industry. We conclude that the number of publications has been growing over the years. However, the absolute number of papers published in all event editions is still not so expressive, especially considering the large number of software testing topics that exist or need improvement. As a result of this work, some points emerge about the relationship of authors and institutions with software testing research.

Keywords: WBMA · Agile testing · Agile methods · Software quality

1 Introduction

Agile methodology has emerged as an alternative to the traditional, sequential way of software development and is also responsible for promoting several changes in how software development organizations work. Instead of following a sequential model, the agile methodology has an iterative and incremental approach, where the product is divided into small parts that are continuously developed and delivered to the customer [1–3].

C. Rocha et al. (Eds.): WBMA 2021, CCIS 1642, pp. 18–31, 2023.
https://doi.org/10.1007/978-3-031-25648-6_2

In 2005 Fowler [4] evidenced that the interest and search for agile methodologies has grown since the early 2000s, this growth in interest for agile methods is due to the success in reducing costs, responsiveness to change, meeting and understanding customer requirements as stated Rising [5], in improving product quality, point out Jain, Sharma, and Ahuja [6] and also processes, such as the testing process, according to Patuci and Morais [7].

Given this context, this work developed a study following the guidelines of a model proposed by Kitchenham [8] in the construction of a Systematic Literature Review (SLR). According to the authors, a systematic approach is predefined using a protocol to identify, evaluate and interpret the available evidence in primary studies related to one or more research questions. This study was inspired on the SLR [9]. Additionally, it was carried out to identify articles available in the literature that present evidence related to new research activities in software testing that can still be developed and discussed in the WBMA.

The structure of this paper is organized as follows. In the Subsect. 2.1 we introduce the event where the papers analyzed here were published, followed by the Subsect. 2.2, where we describe agile testing according to the Agile Manifesto. The Sect. 3 presents the research method used to conduct this study, as well as the steps and questions we aim to answer in this study. The Sect. 4 presents the research results, answering the research questions and analyzing the data. The Sect. 5 shows related and already conducted work that differs from this study. The Sect. 6 discusses the limitations and implications of conducting our analysis. And finally, the Sect. 7 brings implications of our study and points out opportunities for future work.

2 Background

2.1 Brazilian Workshop on Agile Methods

The Brazilian Workshop for Agile Methods (WBMA) is a scientific research track event at the Agile Brazil conference. It is an event about Agile Software development, where during all its editions, they received an expressive number of submissions of research papers from higher education institutions and also papers in partnership with the market, counts with the participation of a large number of students, researchers and professionals from various parts of the world.

One of the primary objectives of the event is to promote greater integration between industry and academia to stimulate the generation of ideas, innovation, and opportunities for all. The main topics of interest at the event are:

- Adoption of Agile/Lean
- Agile Methods for Systems and Software Architecture
- Agile for the Development of Critical Systems
- Human and Social Aspects in Agile Methods
- Agile Project Management, Outsourcing and Governance in the Agile context
- Development in Distributed and Global Agile Teams
- DevOps and Continuous Delivery
- Agile and Lean Teaching and Coaching

- Scaling Agile for Large Corporations
- Experimental Studies in Agile/Lean
- Tools and Techniques in Agile/Lean
- Conceptual Studies and Theoretical Foundations in Agile/Lean
- Technical Debt Management
- Innovation and Agile Entrepreneurship
- Lean Startups
- Agile/Lean in Large and Distributed Teams
- Agile in Government
- Metrics, Measurements and Mining Repositories in Agile contexts
- Patterns and Anti-Patterns in the Agile/Lean application
- User Roles (co-participation)
- Agile Practices and Trends, Evolution and Revolution (Techniques and Management)
- Agile Principles, Lean Manufacturing and other disciplines
- Agile Testing and Quality: Techniques, Standards and Automated Support
- Organizational Transformation and Cultural Aspects in Agile Business
- User Experience (UX) em Agile/Lean
- Test-driven Development
- Refactoring Techniques
- Continuous Inspection Techniques.

However, papers on other topics, as long as they are related to agile methods, are welcome at the event.

The event has space for full papers containing relevant results of original research and for short papers that address ongoing research, experience reports, bibliographic research, or opinion articles [10]. Among the topics of interest, it is relevant for this article to address the papers presented during the ten editions of the Workshop that fall under discussions related to software testing and quality.

2.2   Agile Testing

Software development using agile methodologies promotes severe changes in how software was traditionally built. One of its goals is to demonstrate that functionality is as defined in the requirements and to identify as many bugs as possible. This also includes how development stages are performed, such as software testing [11]. Traditionally people view testing as a phase that happens at the end of development. In agile most have changed it that the chunk of development done is smaller, but the testing still happens last. Nothing has fundamentally changed about how testing is done.

One way to see if this is the case is to ask people about their taskboards. If taskboards have a separate column for testing, it's a sure sign that testing is still being thought of as a phase.

In contrast in agile, testing is just an activity that needs to happen, along with coding, documentation and everything else. Thinking about it like this makes it possible to consider the idea of doing testing tasks before development work. A great way to visualise this on a taskboard is that instead of having a separate column for test, rather just make testing tasks a different colour sticky note. Now put all the tasks in the "To do" column together. Challenge the team to see how many of the testing tasks they can do before any development tasks happen.

For example you can create test cases before any code is written. That way you know how you are going to test it before you build it. You could even create automated acceptance tests first. These should fail since there is no code yet, but once the code is written and the tests pass, the work is done, and there are no test tasks left. Working this way will remove the hurdle of testing always being behind. For some people this is a huge step, however just breaking the mentality that testing tasks follow development is a great start.

Another useful technique is the "Show Me" column. Put it after the "In Progress" column, before the "Done" column. Most teams do code reviews, documentation reviews or even test case reviews on each story. The idea behind the "Show Me" column is to do a review on every task as soon as that task is done. If tasks are small these are micro reviews that might only take a few minutes, but they ensure that at least two people in the team have seen every piece of work, and this can help catch and fix issues much earlier.

Developing quality software is one of the pillars of development in environments that adopt agile methods. These activities have received attention since the beginning of the history of agile development, and many agile practices rely on effective testing [12]. Agile testing is a software testing practice that follows the principles of agile software development [13]. It involves testing activities as early as possible, as stable versions of the code are made available, as agile methods feature incremental product development and delivery [14].

Furthermore, Agile Testing seeks to promote broader thinking about how quality should be adopted and who is responsible for it. Thus, attitudes such as testing at each stage of development instead of just testing at the end; preventing defects from happening instead of having strategies that focus only on finding them; and that the entire Agile team should be responsible for quality instead of just the testers, should always be explored and enhanced [15].

3   Research Method

For this work, we followed the guidelines of a model proposed by Kitchenham [8] in constructing a Systematic Literature Review to develop this mapping study. According to Kitchenham, an SLR is carried out to search for and quantitatively and qualitatively evaluate the studies already conducted in the area that have been published or made available to the scientific community and that have specific academic importance as a basis for research. To this end, it is necessary to determine research questions and, based on these questions, survey the essential data to answer them, thus guiding the reading and selection of articles to select those that will be part of the SLR. It is necessary, therefore, to establish inclusion and exclusion criteria before conducting the research.

The protocol used as a guide throughout the SLR for evidence collection was developed from the formulated questions and these criteria. One of the goals of this work is to present background and, from it, determine which new research activities in software testing can still be developed and discussed in the WBMA. Although it is not an SLR, we adopted the proposed model, so we followed the following phases to conduct this study: Planning and research, Analysis and studies, and Results.

The steps were organized as follows: in Planning and research, we formulated the review questions and defined inclusion and exclusion criteria and search strategy; in Analysis and studies, we performed the selection of studies, analyzed their quality and relevance to our research, and worked on the data extraction process; finally, in the Results step we presented the Analysis and presentation of results, as well as interpreting them.

3.1   Research Questions

One of the essential steps of this analysis activity was the definition of the research questions that led to the search for relevant documents aiming to answer the study's central question: "What is the relevance of the papers published in the WBMA for the testing scenario in Brazil?"

This question was derived from five others with different focuses:

- RQ1. Who are the main authors that have published articles (and other materials) related to software testing at the WBMA?
- RQ2. What are the main institutions that have published articles (and other materials) related to software testing at the WBMA?
- RQ3. What are the main topics discussed at the WBMA related to software testing?
- RQ4. What are the main types of contributions to software testing in the WBMA?
- RQ5. Which articles published in the WBMA related to software testing have the most impact (cited by)?

3.2   Search Strategy, Sources and Selection of Papers

Since we are performing this analysis only on papers published in WBMA events held from 2010 to 2019, we adopted the following inclusion and exclusion criteria:

Inclusion Criteria:

- I1: All papers published in WBMA between 2010 and 2019;
- I2: Articles with software testing topics as the main focus.

Exclusion Criteria:

- E1: All papers that have not been published in the WBMA;
- E2: Papers that were not related to software testing;
- E3: Papers that could not be accessed, even after contacting the authors;

- E4: Papers that are not written in English or Portuguese;
- E5: Presenters' notes, round table papers, workshop reports, invited papers, books presented or released at the event, theses and dissertations;
- E6: Incomplete documents, drafts, presentation slides, and extended abstracts;
- E7: Papers that treat software testing only as part of future work.

A significant number of papers (full papers and short) were published in the WBMA. We followed three filtering or selection steps to arrive at the final result of 12 selected articles. In the first step, we read the titles, abstracts, and keywords and had an initial selection of 22 articles. The data from these articles were organized and listed in a Google spreadsheet[1].

In the next step, the data were extracted from the introduction and conclusion of the works, totaling 18 articles, also listed in a Google spreadsheet[2]. For the final step, the full articles were read and a total of 12 articles were selected, listed in detail in this spreadsheet online[3].

3.3 Data Extraction

The next step in this work is to answer the research questions. For this, the data from the initial 18 articles were extracted and organized, for this, we used a Google spreadsheet (links in session 2.2) and, thus, all the data collected that guided us to this mapping were organized. The information for each article is:

- Identifieritem;
- Title;
- Year of publication;
- Author, Institution and Federal Unit;
- Type of contribution;
- Topics;
- Number of citations;
- Empirical study.

4   Results

This section presents the results that were observed in our study analysis. All articles used to develop the results below respect the inclusion and exclusion criteria in Sect. 2.2. The papers were published in the issues between 2010 and 2019: 1 article in the years 2011, 2013, 2017, and 2018; 2 articles in the years 2010, 2014, 2016, and 2019, totaling 12 articles that are part of this study.

---

[1] https://bit.ly/FiltragemWBMA1.
[2] https://bit.ly/FiltragemWBMA2.
[3] https://bit.ly/ArtigosWBMAFinal.

4.1 RQ1: Which are the Main Authors Who have Published Papers (and Other Materials) Related to Software Testing in the WBMA?

Many authors contributed to the event during the first decade of the WBMA's existence. The selected papers were:

- Contributions from 34 authors;
- Sixteen different institutions (either from industry or academia);
- Six other states in Brazil;
- All regions of the country.

Among the 34 authors, the ones who stood out in the number of papers submitted and accepted at the event are:

- Eduardo Martins Guerra (National Institute for Space Research and Technological Institute of Aeronautics) with three different papers;
- Ivaldir Honório de Farias Junior (the Federal University of Pernambuco and Softex Recife) with two other papers;
- The remaining authors contributed to 1 of the 12 papers analyzed.

Such researchers have been making significant contributions to the community outside of the WBMA, both for their output involving agile methods and software testing, these being:

- Eduardo Martins Guerra has 468 citations in Google Scholar, 303 of them in the last five years, and his most cited article is focused on software testing. Information is taken from his Google Scholar profile page[4];
- Ivaldir Honório de Farias Junior also has essential studies in the area of testing and agile methods; his Google Scholar profile shows that among his most cited articles are studies done on software testing[5].

The complete list of authors and their test-related papers published in the WBMA can be seen in the spreadsheet[6]. These data have been organized in Table 1.

Table 1. Authors who have published the most in WBMA

Author	Papers	#	%
Eduardo Martins Guerra	WBMA02, WBMA07, WBMA10	3	25%
Ivaldir Honório de Farias Junior	WBMA08, WBMA12	2	16.7%

---

[4] https://bit.ly/AuthorGuerra.
[5] https://bit.ly/AuthorIvaldir.
[6] https://bit.ly/WBMAAutores.

4.2   RQ2: What are the Main Institutions that have Published Articles (and Other Materials) Related to Software Testing at the WBMA?

Analyzing Table 2, among the 16 institutions (industry and academia) that published, the Federal University of Pernambuco stands out, which published 3 of the 12 articles selected in this study, followed by the institutions Federal University of São Paulo, Federal Technological University of Paraná and National Institute for Space Research, with 2 published articles each. The other 12 institutions collaboratively participated in the production of 1 article each.

Consistent with the results of RQ1, UFPE has as a member of its team the researcher Ivaldir Honório de Farias Junior, one of the authors with the highest number of publications in the event. Besides, UFPE's graduate program in Computer Science has the maximum CAPES concept (grade 7), which may contribute to the strong presence of UFPE in the event.

Table 2. Institutions that published the most in the WBMA

Institution	Published papers
Federal University of Pernambuco	WBMA06, WBMA08, WBMA12
Federal University of São Paulo	WBMA02, WBMA10
Federal Technological University of Paraná	WBMA09, WBMA11
National Institute for Space Research	WBMA07, WBMA10
National Center for Natural Disaster Monitoring and Alert	WBMA07
CESAR School	WBMA08
Group Being Educational	WBMA10
Nokia Institute of Technology	WBMA03
Aeronautical Technological Institute	WBMA02
Pontifical Catholic University of Rio Grande do Sul	WBMA05
Softex Recife	WBMA08
University of Campinas	WBMA04
University of São Paulo	WBMA01
Mato Grosso State University	WBMA08
Federal University of São Carlos	WBMA10
Federal University of Amazonas	WBMA03

There were contributions from 6 states and five regions of the country:

- São Paulo is the state with the most significant number of publications, 5 in total;
- Pernambuco, with 3 publications;
- Paraná with 2 publications;
- Rio Grande do Sul, Mato Grosso and Amazonas contributed with 1 paper each.

Figures 1 and 2 show these state and region distributions, respectively.

Fig. 1. Contribution to the WBMA by state

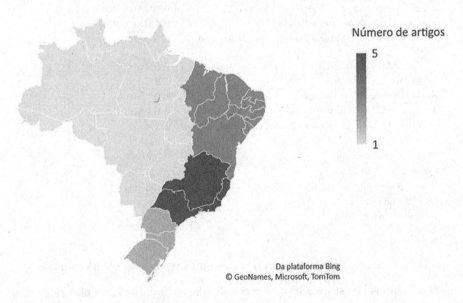

Fig. 2. Contribution to the WBMA by region

4.3 RQ3: Which Articles Published in the WBMA Related to Software Testing have the Most Impact (Cited By)?

The answer to this question can be obtained by checking the keywords in the articles surveyed. It is important to note that some articles do not have keywords and that even if they do, they may not be enough to categorize our research in a way that clarifies the main idea of the articles. As we also verified a certain redundancy in the keyword definitions of some articles, we decided to define the main topics according to what we proved to be the general idea of each work, respecting the fact that they may address more than one of the defined topics.

Thus, we observed that the most covered topics were:

- "Study of Agile Methodologies in Testing," cited by 7 of the published papers, representing 58.33% of the papers;
- "Adaptation to the agile model," cited by 6 of the published papers, representing 50% of the papers;
- "Test Support Tool/Framework" cited in 4 of the submitted papers, corresponding to 33.33%.

This data shows that the first two topics address the agile model, where 3 of the papers appear in both.

In addition to these 3 points above, if we look at all the topics in more than one article, we can see five significant issues being addressed among the papers used for this study. The complete listing of articles is described in Table 3.

Table 3. Most discussed topics among the papers published at the WBMA

Topics	Papers	Total	%
Study of agile methodologies in testing	WBMA004, WBMA005, WBMA006, WBMA008, WBMA010, WBMA011, WBMA012	7	58.3%
Adaptation to the agile model	WBMA001, WBMA003, WBMA004, WBMA006, WBMA010, WBMA009	6	50%
Test Support Tool/Framework	WBMA001, WBMA002, WBM007, WBM009	4	33.3%
Test process management (Metrics, Bugs)	WBMA003, WBMA001, WBMA009	3	25%
Improvements for code annotations	WBMA002, WBMA007	2	16.7%

4.4 RQ4: What are the Main Types of Contributions to Software Testing in the WBMA?

The answer to this question can be obtained by considering how the authors have classified their articles. The list with this classification can be seen in the "Type of contribution" tab of the spreadsheet[7]. The idea behind this question is to answer the contributions of these papers published within the WBMA to software testing. Thus, it was found that the three main types of contributions of the analyzed papers were:

– Improvements (of processes or practices) with 4 articles;
– Use Experience (of type of process applied, application domain or purpose) and Tools with 3 articles.

The complete list (Table 4) also includes Best Practices followed by Definition, containing 1 article. One can infer that, during the ten years of the WBMA, there was a great concern on the part of the authors in contributing to the maturing of the, by then, new agile model, seeking to support its adhesion and constantly worrying about its impact on how the software testing process would be carried out.

Table 4. Main types of contributions to the WBMA

Type of contribution	Papers
Improvements (of processes or practices)	WBMA03, WBMA04, WBMA11, WBMA12
User experience	WBMA06, WBMA08, WBMA09
Tools	WBMA01, WBMA02, WBM07
Best practices	WBMA10
Definições	WBMA05

5 Related Work

The Brazilian Workshop on Agile Methodologies study focused on software testing has not been developed so far; no similar studies were found in any of the bibliographic bases we used. This study contributes to the analysis of the WBMA, the authors, and the different topics related to software testing and identifies which areas still need study and which still have gaps even though researched. As well as a comparison of the progress of the studies in these ten years of existence.

---

[7] https://bit.ly/WBMAAutores.

6   Limitations and Threats

The study carried out presented significant limitations regarding its sample, these being:

- The sample would be the papers on testing during the ten years of the event, there were different topics presented within the large area of testing, so we could not perform many comparative studies on the progress of a particular area during this period;
- Another limitation that directly impacts the research results is the lack of studies on important topics in the area of software testing;
- Finally, another significant limitation is the sample size, which presents a reduced number of articles and allows us to consider the results found only for the population in question.

7   Conclusion and Future Works

In this paper, we reviewed which are the software testing-related papers published at WBMA during the ten years of the event and what were their contributions to the community. We could present some information that can be used to provide people with a more detailed analysis of these papers to understand how much they have contributed to the evolution of software testing, always pointing in a better direction.

Section 2 provides the results of our mapping, where the most active authors and institutions showing participation and interest in the topics related to this field of study are shown in detail. It is essential to highlight the issues that appeared the most in our survey: Improvements (of processes or practices), Experience of Use (of type of process applied, application domain or purpose), and Tools.

Through this survey, we could notice the community's desires during these 10 years, how to adapt to an agile context and how to insert software testing in this transformation process, either by new tools or by modifying the current process. This paper presents an overview of the importance of the event in Brazil and the positive impacts for the study of software testing.

In future work, we consider that a similar analysis in the other areas addressed by the WBMA could help define an understanding of the event's impact on the Brazilian community, which areas need more investment in research and primary research opportunities.

Primary Studies

In this section, we present the articles initially listed for this study (Table 5):

Table 5. Primary studies

ES01	ATMM uma ferramenta para gerenciamento de metricas de teste no contexto de métodos ágeis (2010)
ES02	ClassMock: A Testing Tool for Reflective Classes Which Consume Code Annotations (2010)
ES03	Uma Abordagem Empírica para o Tratamento de Bugs em Ambientes Ágeis (2011)
ES04	Incremental Tests: An Approach to Improve Software Tests in Agile Teams (2012)
ES05	Experiencia bem-sucedida de adocão de Metodos Ágeis em uma Empresa Pública de Tecnologia da Informação e Comunicação: um relato preliminar (2013)
ES06	Applying Continuous Integration principles in safety critical airborne software (2014)
ES07	On The Understanding of Agile Methods and Their Practice in Brazil (2014)
ES08	Using nokia test to evaluating quality and productivity on scrum-CMMI environments (2014)
ES09	Critical Factors in Agile Software Projects according to People, Process and Technology Perspective (2015)
ES10	What is Agile, Which Practices are Used, and Which Skills are Necessary according to Brazilian Professionals: Findings of an Initial Survey (2015)
ES11	ReTest: Framework for Applying TDD in the Development of Non-deterministic Algorithm (2016)
ES12	Quality Assurance in Agile Software Development: A Systematic Review (2016)
ES13	Meta-modelo para rastreabilidade de requisitos e análise de impacto nos métodos ágeis (2017)
ES14	Qual o cenário atual da pesquisa em metodologias ágeis? (2017)
ES15	Agile Testing in Brazil: A Systematic Mapping (2018)
ES16	A Tool to Measure Test Driven Development Compliance: A Case Study with Professionals (2018)
ES17	An Empirical Study of Test-Driven Development vs. Test-Last Development Using Eye Tracking (2019)
ES18	A Survey on Agile Practices and Challenges of a Global Software Development Team (2019)

References

1. Dingsøyr, T., Lassenius, C.: Emerging themes in agile software development: introduction to the special section on continuous value delivery. Inf. Softw. Technol. **77**, 56–60 (2016). http://www.sciencedirect.com/science/article/pii/S0950584916300829
2. de Gois Marques, D., Dallégrave, T.L.D.A., Barbosa, L.E.L., de Oliveira Rodrigues, C.M., Santos, W.B.: Industry-academy collaboration in agile methodology: a systematic literature review. In: 2022 17th Iberian Conference on Information Systems and Technologies (CISTI), pp. 1–6 (2022)
3. Santos, W.B., Cunha, J.A.O.G., Moura, H., Margaria, T.: Towards a theory of simplicity in agile software development: a qualitative study. In: 2017 43rd Euromicro Conference on Software Engineering and Advanced Applications (SEAA), pp. 40–43 (2017)
4. Fowler, M.: The New Methodology (2005). http://martinfowler.com/articles/newMethodology.html. Accessed 4 May 2020
5. Rising, L., Janoff, N.S.: The scrum software development process for small teams. IEEE Softw. **17**(4), 26–32 (2000)
6. Jain, P., Sharma, A., Ahuja, L.: The impact of agile software development process on the quality of software product. In: 2018 7th International Conference on Reliability, Infocom Technologies and Optimization (Trends and Future Directions) (ICRITO), pp. 812–815 (2018)
7. Patuci, R.L.O.M.G.O.: Incremental tests: an approach to improve software tests in agile teams. In: 3rd Brazilian Workshop on Agile Methods (WBMA 2012), vol. 3, pp. 61–71 (2012)
8. Kitchenham, B.: Procedures for performing systematic reviews, vol. 33. Keele University, Keele, UK, August 2004
9. Melo, A., Fagundes, R., Lenarduzzi, V., Santos, W.B.: Identification and measurement of requirements technical debt in software development: a systematic literature review. J. Syst. Softw. 111483 (2022). https://www.sciencedirect.com/science/article/pii/S0164121222001650
10. WBMA 2019 - Agile Brazil (2019). Accessed 23 July 2020. https://www.agilebrazil.com/2019/docs/pt/wbma/
11. Beck, K., et al.: Manifesto for agile software development (2001). http://www.agilemanifesto.org/
12. Vanderburg, G.: A simple model of agile software processes - or - extreme programming annealed, vol. 40, pp. 539–545, October 2005
13. Bach, J., Bolton, M.: Rapid software testing, version (1.3.2) (2007). www.satisficc.com
14. Talby, D., Keren, A., Hazzan, O., Dubinsky, Y.: Agile software testing in a large-scale project. IEEE Softw. **23**(4), 30–37 (2006)
15. Crispin, L., Gregory, J.: Agile Testing: A Practical Guide for Testers and Agile Teams. Pearson Education (2009)

Assuring the Evolvability of Legacy Systems in Devops Transformation/Adoption: Insights of an Experience Report

Álax Alves(✉) and Carla Rocha

Universidade de Brasília - Campus Gama, Gama, Distrito Federal, Brazil
alaxallves@gmail.com, caguiar@unb.br

Abstract. DevOps has changed the software industry to enable continuous delivery. While many studies have investigated on how to introduce DevOps into a software product from the organizational perspective, less is known about the technical challenges developers and practitioners face when transforming legacy codes into DevOps, despite the undisputed importance of this topic. In this paper, throughout the context of web applications, we report the results of a study case with the adoption of four legacy open-source projects into DevOps to understand which refactoring techniques and strategies influence developers' decisions. We analyze two dependent variables: the technique used and how they are applied to the project. After every implementation, there was an overview of the process that just occurred and later a written report on how the strategies have been applied, their respective order, which strategy has been more fruitful, and such. Those reports have been the foundation of this study. The main findings of such study are that some strategies are more efficient when viewed from the evolution aspect and the sequence these techniques are employed matter.

Keywords: Devops · Refactoring · Program comprehension · Study cases · Experience report

1 Introduction and Motivation

DevOps combines cultural philosophies, practices, and tools that increase an organization's ability to deliver applications and services at high velocity: evolving and improving products faster than organizations using traditional software development and infrastructure management processes. This speed enables organizations to serve their customers better and compete more effectively in the market [7].

As more companies adopt DevOps to improve their workflow and productivity, many challenges related to the infrastructure and the legacy software systems have arisen. DevOps is about people and processes [24]. It is a methodology that enables organizational groups to communicate with each other across

© Springer Nature Switzerland AG 2023
C. Rocha et al. (Eds.): WBMA 2021, CCIS 1642, pp. 32–53, 2023.
https://doi.org/10.1007/978-3-031-25648-6_3

silos and to coordinate their activities. Thus, it is not surprising that established cultural habits are the number one challenge to DevOps, especially barriers to cross-organizational collaboration, the critical element of successful DevOps practice [22].

Legacy codes are usually characterized by the following: use of outdated frameworks, no test (neither unit nor integration), no containerization, no automation tools, nonexistence of technical documentation, monolithic architecture, no continuous integration, no automation at all.

The professionals working on a legacy system have to put in extra effort to refactor it, especially legacy systems. There are no strategies in place for implementation of refactoring techniques. No plans designed to guide the developers with the same. Developers performing with their own knowledge and sometimes ended up messing with the code [23].

Outdated legacy applications usually work tied to running a production service that tends to be manual, repetitive, automatable, tactical, devoid of enduring value, and that scales linearly as a service grows [26]. While cloud applications are needed for quick application delivery, some legacy systems cannot be integrated, leaving the IT infrastructure out of sync and incapable of operating at a fast pace [2]. The solutions to such legacy challenges are often time-consuming, or costly [2]. All this is stated still considering the web applications spectrum.

Evolvability is a vital software aspect, and fundamental to its existence. It motivates software engineering researches, and practices [29]. 'Evolution consists of repeated software changes. Defined software change processes lead to improved productivity and quality of software evolution' [29].

Microservices is an important architectural style that prioritizes evolvability. Evolvability is especially crucial for software with frequently changing requirements, internet-based systems for instance. Software professionals apply a set of numerous activities that we refer to as evolvability assurance [9]. These activities are usually of analytical nature to identify issues or a constructive nature to remediate issues. That includes techniques like code review or refactoring, standardization, guidelines, conscious technical debt management, and tools, metrics, or patterns [9].

Thus, in the appropriate context, migrating monolithic architectures to microservices could bring in many benefits including, but not limited to, flexibility to adapt to the technological changes in order to avoid technology lock-in, and more importantly, reduced time-to-market [8].

Legacy apps are typically harder to adopt DevOps due to a blend of technology, process and cultural issues. The cultural issue regard to the initial resistance from teams to move into DevOps ways is due to reluctance to change, emerging from an inertia of doing things a certain way for years if not decades. Most of these systems were not built for the agile workflows that focus on incremental and iterative deliveries. Amidst challenges like too much technical debt, tightly integrated hardware components, fragile codebase, it is tough to select specialised approach like DevOps.

While designing and developing a greenfield project, architects and developers start afresh and have the opportunity to take into consideration the requirements of DevOps [30]. In case of legacy systems, which have evolved over a period of time without any consideration of automation, the adoption of the DevOps approach may result in large-scale refactoring or redesign. It may prove to be a significant challenge to automate the vast amount of legacy code and processes [30].

Considering tests and their automation, Legacy systems tend to have low code coverage due to few or no unit tests. Testing is typically done in higher environments and is manual. As more features are added to a legacy system, the manual testing effort increases drastically, eventually slowing down feature delivery. This problem is amplified when there are multiple teams working on the same code base [30].

The challenge is identifying which tool and concept are adequate to the context. As in any software process improvement initiative, the path to a successful DevOps implementation is unique to each organization. Still, it is possible to learn from challenges experienced during other process adoptions in order to plan future initiatives [34].

In this work, we report the results of a study case with the adoption of four legacy open-source web projects into DevOps to understand which refactoring techniques and strategies influence developers' decisions. We map the refactoring techniques used, the sequence they were employed, the benefits perceived by the organization, and the challenges faced by developers when deploying each refactoring technique. We analyse the project repositories, the commits, the issues discussions, the communication channels. We present a set of lessons learned, with the DevOps benefits for each refactoring technique experimented, the impact of the order the techniques are employed from developers perspective and some guidelines for legacy projects aiming at adopting DevOps .

2   Related Works

Although there have been several discussions on DevOps practices and how they benefit one's project, applying such practices to an existing project is often painful.

When it comes to refactoring legacy code with focus on DevOps, S.A.M. Rizvi and Zeba Khanam have proposed methodology [31]. Their article proposes a methodology that can be employed to apply the refactoring activities on the legacy system, employing the aspect-oriented techniques. Considering the refactoring activities that are more likely to improve the software design and quality, the developers should adopt an approach that would focus on a restricted set of refactoring patterns. Thus allowing the developers to choose their desired set of strategies [31].

Gangadhar Hari Rao proposes a roadmap for implementing DevOps in a legacy software, with focus on building a CD pipeline with the supporting capabilities. With this roadmap Rao concludes that the successful adoption of the DevOps methodology for a legacy system is possible only if the teams working on legacy systems also change their processes and mindset towards Agile and CD.

In each stage of the roadmap he considers the challenges and proposes actions to overcome them, always with a great focus on CD - what could involve great costs, depending on the legacy system to be considered [30].

Chia-Chu Chiang and Coskun Bayrak propose a refactoring strategy that consists of converting legacy systems into component-based systems. The process involves program understanding, business rules extraction, and software transformation. In their paper, they present a semi-automated program slicing technique for business rules extraction from legacy code and convert the reusable code into a component conforming to the protocols of a component interconnection model [11].

Errickson-Connor [17] also proposed a strategy that consisted of steps of a software modernization process where a legacy code is transformed into new languages and new environments. She suggests that a legacy code needs to be cleaned up, such as removing program anomalies before being transformed. The next stage involves software restructuring tasks such as isolating business rules, identifying business rules, and extracting business rules as reusable services. When the code corresponding to a business rule is extracted, it is ready for transformation into components in stage three. The final stage is to manage these reusable components in a software environment.

Regarding implementing certain levels of DevOps in legacy software, the SmartSheet website ensures Virtualization and, consequently, Microservices as core practices. Working with small, reusable building blocks of code ensures that the application under development is not affected by the increase in deployments' velocity in the DevOps environment. Containers are the next evolutionary step in virtualization technology [6].

Finally, Leonardo Leite, Carla Rocha, Fabio Kon, Dejan Milojicic, and Paulo Meirelles in their work A Survey of DevOps Concepts and Challenges outline a conceptual framework to guide engineers, managers, and academics in the exploration of DevOps tools, implications, and challenges. The conceptual framework is composed of conceptual maps, which are diagrams structured as graphs in which nodes depict concepts and arrows represent relationships among concepts [24].

Their survey investigates the DevOps concepts and challenges from multiple perspectives: engineers, managers, and researchers. Also explores a much broader range of sources. More up-to-date concepts of DevOps and its tools are analyzed, categorized and correlates to the DevOps concepts, and discuss which roles in the organization should use which tools. It concludes by summarizing and discussing some of the main DevOps challenges [24].

3   Background

3.1   DevOps - Practices and Strategies

DevOps is a software development and delivery process that helps in emphasizing communication along with cross-functional collaboration between product management, software development, and operations professionals. Also widely considered a collaborative and multidisciplinary organizational effort to automate continuous delivery of new software updates while guaranteeing their correctness and reliability [24].

From the technical perspective, DevOps relies heavily on automation tools, including tools for container management, continuous integration, orchestration, monitoring, deployment, and testing [36]. Automated deployment pipelines and monitoring facilitate error detection. The micro-services architectural style is quickly becoming the standard for building continuously integrated and deployed systems. DevOps aims to achieve some business outcomes, such as reducing risk and cost, complying with regulations, and improving product quality and customer satisfaction [24].

DevOps is an evolution of the agile movement, it proposes a complementary set of agile practices to enable the iterative delivery of software in short cycles effectively. Besides automating the delivery process, DevOps initiatives have also focused on using automated runtime monitoring for improving software runtime properties, such as performance, scalability, availability, and resilience [24].

Using containers, one could run a single container to execute a small micro-service or software process to a more extensive application [20]. Containers and micro-services enable DevOps [24]. Considering a hypothetical context, running a micro-service on bare metal is an attractive option, since multiple services on a single operating system instance can lead to conflicting library versions; one micro-service failure could affect others' behavior.

Regarding DevOps practices, Continuous Testing (CT) highlights as the most fitting concept with two of the core aspects of DevOps, continuity of the process of development and a source of uninterrupted feedback - despite being a relatively new concept in Software Engineering. The practice of Continuous Testing pivots around test automation as well as early and frequent testing. Continuous Testing is a crucial component of the software development cycle that includes continuous development, integration, and deployment.

Whereas some authors say microservices facilitate effective implementation of DevOps, others say microservices require DevOps, since deployment automation minimizes the overhead to manage a significant number of microservices. However, adopting microservices comes with several challenges. First, there is heterogeneity in non-functional patterns such as "startup scripts, configuration files, administration endpoints, and logging locations". Technological heterogeneity can be a productivity barrier for newcomers in the team. Second, microservices must be deployed to production with the same set of versions used for integration tests [24].

3.2   Legacy Software and Its Challenges

Legacy software is commonly defined as an application that is no longer updated or supported by the developer. Likewise, the software can become legacy if the developer's operation ceases or bought by another entity that decides to throw it out [12]. The definition is not limited to that, Legacy software systems are also considered programs that are still well used by the community or have some potential inherent value but were developed years, days, or even hours ago [21]. A software becomes legacy when its dependencies are not keeping up with the latest updates. That could represent software developed a few days ago, which has a vast and active maintainer community.

According to Sommerville [35], Legacy systems can be rawly defined as old software systems that are used by an organization and usually rely on obsolete technology but are still essential to the business. This definition is totally correct, but coming to a wider definition legacy software also represents a software created one day ago. That is justified given the rapid advances and the increased reliance on software-related technologies [10].

Often legacy codes have been maintained and developed by hundreds of programmers. While many changes have been made to it, the supporting documentation may not be current, and the programming style does not follow current standards [21]. The challenges could get more prominent, as such software might offer a volatile development environment - which makes contributing at any level very hard. Those challenges could be not have a representative test coverage or an arduous setup of the work environment.

A very proper example of legacy software is the web-based social platform Noosfero [13]. Basically Noosfero is an open source framework for social networking. Considering that its first versions are dated back to 2007 it has several legacy practices and code.

Including DevOps into a large-scale legacy system day-to-day is a challenging exercise since they often predate DevOps or may have been developed without taking into account the unique characteristics of its practices.

DevOps principles, practices, and tools are changing the software industry. However, many industry practitioners, both engineers and managers, are still not aware of how their daily work can be affected by such principles, practices, and tools. As well, some legacy architectures might not be designed to run automated tests. Nonetheless, teams must be aware that cultural factors, such as managers who say "This is the way we have always done it", can limit the adoption of continuous delivery more than technical factors. [24].

Although companies recognize the importance of automated testing, they still struggle to implement it fully. Other factors that make automated testing complex are hardware availability for load testing and user experiment assessment. The benefits delivered by a deployment pipeline, that is continuous delivery, are many. However, engineers must be aware that setting up the infrastructure for continuous deployment can demand a considerable effort. Breaking down the system into microservices also requires building multiple pipelines [24].

There are still many open questions about how organizations should adopt DevOps. It is stated that DevOps adoption requires top-management support. Sometimes it does not happen in the first moment, and an anti-organizational strategy can take place. Moreover, arguments to encourage DevOps adoption can differ from engineers to managers - which is the organizational hierarchy structure of most legacy code teams [24].

4   Strategies to Bring DevOps into Legacy Code

Refactoring is the process of changing a software system so that it does not alter the code's external behavior yet improves its internal structure. It is a disciplined way to clean up code that minimizes the chances of introducing bugs. In essence, when one refactors actually is improving the design of the code after it has been written [18].

In the context of Legacy Code involves embracing several strategies and practices. Considering the challenges involved in refactoring legacy code, several organizations are not rushing to adopt such practices properly.

It is important to mention that the techniques, or strategies, described below in this work will not be considered refactoring strategies - analyzing through the spectrum of SOLID and Clean Code set of techniques. In this context, F the following strategies are considered to be strategies simply required to a legacy software team to adopt the DevOps culture.

4.1   Legacy in the Box

Legacy code, especially massive monoliths, is one of the most unsatisfying, high-friction experiences for developers. Although there is always much caution involved in extending and maintaining legacy monoliths, such upgrades continue to prove to be very necessary, even though it takes a lot of work and money to keep maintaining such monolith.

To help reduce the friction, developers have used virtualized machine images or container images with Docker containers to create immutable images of legacy systems and their configurations. This technique, called "legacy in the box", contain the legacy code in a box for developers to run locally and remove the need for rebuilding, re-configuring or sharing environments. In an ideal scenario, teams that own legacy systems generate the corresponding boxed legacy images through their build pipelines, and developers can then run and orchestrate these images in their allocated sandbox more reliably.

Adopting Legacy in the Box practice is not only about wrapping the legacy code in a container and ship it. It also features some other DevOps-related practices, such as adopting Continuous Integration and Continuous Deploy (CI/CD) into the project workflow - previously described.

For instance, when it comes to adopting Continuous Integration into the Legacy project, a core practice consists of all developers committing to the mainline branch daily. When a team makes changes in smaller increments and integrates them into the mainline regularly. More minor changes, shipped to production quickly, are a lot easier to debug when something breaks. Rather than living in branches for long chunks of time, changes are continuously integrated [25].

Beyond version control, a continuous integration server is one of the more essential tools a development team can put to fair use. A continuous integration server is unbiased. Its tasks boil down to telling the team whether the most recent changes still pass the stages it is configured to run [25].

The last step of a fully automated build is deploying to production, which requires an automated deployment process that every developer should be able to run, just like the continuous integration server. With an automated build in place, everyone can deploy to staging or production, anytime [25].

4.2   Testing, Integrating and Deploying Continuously

As previously said, CI/CD is a method to frequently deliver apps to customers by introducing automation into the stages of app development. Such practices introduce ongoing automation and continuous monitoring throughout the software life-cycle, from integration and testing phases to delivery and deployment. Taken together, these connected practices are often referred to as a CI/CD pipeline [1].

When Continuous Testing is adequately implemented, an organization can get a constant insight into the robustness of the latest software build and ensure speedy delivery of high-quality software. CI/CD is a method to frequently deliver apps to customers by introducing automation into app development stages. Continuous Integration helps teams work more efficiently because the different components of a complex system will more assuredly work together. By having each piece of code verified by an automated build, a team is allowed to develop cohesive software more rapidly. Leading to significantly reduced integration problems and quick error detection. However, once this bottleneck is overcome, CD presents several benefits that directly influence the end product. Since CD - and CI - are all about automation, it allows teams to focus on the actual product and testing. Also, make it possible to integrate teams and processes with a unified pipeline, thus standardizing the entire project.

Continuous practices are expected to provide several benefits such as: getting more and quick feedback from the software development process and customers; having frequent and reliable releases, which lead to improved customer satisfaction and product quality; through CD, the connection between development and operations teams is strengthened and manual tasks can be eliminated.

In DevOps, CI/CD along with testing plays a vital role since it results in trustful services due to the use of agile development methods and concepts - also embraced by the DevOps practices. Continuous integration tools orchestrate several automated actions that, together, implement the deployment pipeline pattern. Among the stages orchestrated by the pipeline are: package generation, automated test execution for correctness verification, and deployment to both development and production environments [24].

Continuous Delivery has been the approach to bring automation, quality, and discipline to create a reliable and repeatable process to release software into production. Pillars of DevOps : automated stages, quality, repeatable process, automated test stages, and more [32].

Continuous delivery and continuous deployment will be used as synonyms, also referred to as CD. CD usually means a developer's application changes are automatically bug tested and uploaded to a repository, where it can be later deployed to a live production environment. Another approach to defining CD is that it can refer to automatically releasing a developer's changes from the repository to production, where it is made available to customers. It addresses the problem of overloading operations teams with manual processes that slow down app delivery. CI/CD is really a process, often visualized as a pipeline, that involves adding a high degree of ongoing automation and continuous monitoring to app development [1].

4.3 Architecture

A Software Architecture is concerned with both structure and behavior, is concerned with significant decisions only, may conform to an architectural style, is influenced by its stakeholders and its environment, and embodies decisions based on rationale. Some authors explore software design in the context of DevOps, continuous delivery, and continuous deployment. However, developers may still struggle with this in practice, since achieving the desired architecture can be infeasible in a single first DevOps [24].

As well as defining structural elements, an architecture defines the interactions between these structural elements. And are these interactions that provide the desired system behavior [16].

Micro-services. When it comes to specifying among the various architectures, the micro-services architecture stands out to aid the DevOps implementation. As the size of a software systems increases, the computation algorithms and data structures no longer constitute the major design problems. When systems are constructed from many components, the overall system's organization - the software architecture - presents a new set of design problems [19].

Micro-services is a style of architecture that emphasizes dividing the system into small and lightweight services that are purposely built to perform a very cohesive business function and is an evolution of the traditional service-oriented architecture style. This architecture is an approach to developing an application as a set of small independent services. Each of the services is running in its independent process [27]. As the software grows, it can be a great approach to achieve scalability.

5   The Case Study

The previous section described several handy concepts that, when explored, could represent a great advantage when refactoring a legacy code. Such concepts obey a particular pattern when applied to the process of upgrading and also refactoring itself.

In order to successfully achieve this work's goal, there should be defined as a well-structured process, specifically, agile developing methodologies.

5.1   Open Source Software (OSS)

Open source software is software with source code that anyone can inspect, modify and enhance [28]. Open source software can be defined as software distributed under a licensing agreement which allows the source code (computer code) to be shared, viewed, and modified by other users and organizations [33].

Freedom with the source code allows developers to create unique solutions, which can then be built upon by other community members. This process of "crowdsourcing" allows for development shops to pull beyond their teams' talents and access a repository of information compiled by the community at large.

Open source solutions geared toward the enterprise often have thriving communities around them, bound by a shared drive to support and improve a solution that both the enterprise and the community benefit from (and believe in). The global communities united around improving these solutions introduce new concepts and capabilities faster, better, and more effectively than internal teams working on proprietary solutions. Not to mention that this brings several benefits to the end-user as well.

Furthermore, utilizing DevOps solutions in the context of an open-source community can be both time and cost-effective and also very practical to organizations in general. DevOps is a newer and less mature software practice. It requires a new tool, process, and solutions development; in other words, the developers will empirically implement the DevOps strategies according to its organizational needs. Leveraging open source solutions can expedite that process. Many of the key DevOps tools used today either are or started as open-source solutions for DevOps problems, which certainly fits an open-source software project's objectives. While DevOps and open source are two entirely separate things, though, the reality is that it's difficult to separate the two at this point. Many open source projects rely on DevOps tools and principles, and DevOps depends heavily on open source applications as both the glue that binds it all together and the engine that keeps everything moving [3].

Open-source software development, particularly its core tenets of collaboration and transparency, has always been an integral part of DevOps. This is one of the reasons that DevOps tends to be an easier adjustment for developers, who tend to have experience with open-source software and its concepts and technologies [5].

With OSS, community members have open access to the source code and can use it in any way they see fit. Also, an open-source project can be altered and extended by any developer familiar with the source code. This grants organizations freedom and long-term viability because hundreds of developers supporting a widely adopted OSS project can be called upon long into the future.

5.2   Study Design

Methodology. Ethnography is a research method designed to describe and analyze the social life and culture of a specific social system [15]. The central tenet of this approach is to understand values, beliefs, or ideas shared for a group under study from the members' point of view. For this, the ethnographer needs to become a member of the group, observing in detail what people actually do and learning their language, social norms, rules, and artifacts.

Table 1. Study cases information

Project	Mapknitter	Noosfero	Spectral workbench	Salicml
Number of commits	2,512 commits	16,785 commits	1,271 commits	638 commits
Contributors	75 contributors	25 contributors	18 contributors	14 contributors
Lines of source code	60.863 lines	227.024 lines	46.201 lines	85.804 lines
Date of first commit	26/04/2009	27/06/2007	27/09/2010	27/03/2018
License	GPL v3	GPL v3	GPL v3	GPL v3
Main programming language	Ruby	Ruby	Ruby	Python
Framework version	Rails 3.2.2	Rails 4.2.4	Rails 3.2.3	Django 2.2

Ethnographic research is a qualitative methodology which requires the researcher to interpret the real world from the perspective of the informers in the investigation [14]. And in software engineering context, it can strengthen investigations of social and human aspects in the software development process since the significance of these aspects of software practice is already well-established.

In this work, we acquire data by using the ethnographic research method of participant observation and documentation analysis. The participant observation method makes it possible to explain and justify the meaning of the experiences through the experience of the observer and allow the informant to judge what is important rather than what he thinks is important. In addition to sensitivity, the observer needs to interpret what is happening in the community around him.

Software developers find it easier to reveal the processes present in their thoughts when communicating with other software developers, which makes this communication a valuable opportunity to observe the development process. This justifies why in this work, a method for data collection used was keep track of the various communication tools used to exchange information regarding certain project.

Contextualized Methodology. This study methodology has been fundamental in the context of this work. Through it, it has been possible to collect every needed data that has been later used to build the strategies/techniques. By observing and describing the entire process of implementing the DevOps culture in a legacy project, it was possible to obtain very relevant data that has been used to generate the DevOps strategies and their order of implementation.

There were four study cases conducted as shown in Table 1, each case had its our peculiarities which has allowed us to apply a different approach at every study. Each case study consisted in contributing to an open-source software community in terms of applying certain strategies to get the community to embrace the DevOps culture and practices.

The first case was Noosfero, an open-source framework for social networking that has around fourteen years since its first commit, nearly two hundred and fifty thousand lines of code, twenty thousand commits and twenty-five contributors - the most legacy of all cases. The second case analyzed was Mapknitter, which is a project that is part of a huge ecosystem of services provided by the PublicLab community, it allows geographical data exporting and uploading, with around seventy-five contributors, sixty thousand lines of code and eleven years old. The third study case conducted was Spectral Workbench, which is also part of the PublicLab ecosystem, a web based application to collect, archive, share, and analyze spectral data. It has eighteen contributors, twelve hundred commits and around forty-six thousand of lines.

In order to get a possible different point of view, the fourth case was conducted mainly by Victor Moura. It consisted in the project Salicml, that has around eighty-five thousand lines of code, fourteen contributors and over six hundred commits. Salicml is a web application that processed business indicators from cultural projects and presented them in a web dashboard.

In each project, the study has lasted 5–6 months, including the one conducted by Victor Moura. The only exception to this has been the Noosfero case, in which the it has lasted around a year - as it is the bigger project in number of lines.

As more studies have been conducted the pattern of strategies to be applied were becoming more and more clear. During every case, it was noticed that before starting any framework upgrade, it would be indispensable to cover the project of tests. However, to test it properly, it would also be fascinating to know which parts of the code I would be testing and how much of the project I would be testing, that is, in percentage. Also, a smart idea would be automating the entire test process since it increases the number of times exponentially one has to trigger the command to run the tests.

All of this empirical work done in various legacy projects leads us to conclude that before adopting Continuous Integration, one should adopt Continuous Testing before it. The interesting part is that every strategy has been obtained through this, making the Case Study methodology very important for this work accomplishment.

It is also worth mentioning that after the first case study conducted - Noosfero - there was already a solid set of practices to-become-strategies and their most adequate usage order. As there were more study cases, the strategies became more and more evident and their order.

After the completion of every study case every information source was analyzed, as commits, issue reports, pull requests, informal communication tools and such. By analyzing that kind of resource it was possible building the set of practices, called Strategies in this paper. These resources also made possible gathering the posthumous lessons learned from the cases experiences, that would later become the foundation for this study.

6   Results

In Table 2, it is objectively pointed out which strategy and its order of usage to every case during the study. The following sections details more about each case (Table 3).

Table 2. Strategies per study case

Project	Repository link	Description	Technique applied (in order of usage)
Noosfero	https://gitlab.com/ noosfero/noosfero/	An open-source framework for social networking with blogs, e-Portfolios, CMS, RSS, thematic discussion, events scheduling, and more	Continuous integration, legacy in the box
Mapknitter	https://github.com/ publiclab/ mapknitter/	A free and open-source software created run by Public Lab. It lets people upload their own aerial images in a web interface over some existing map data, share it, and export for print	Legacy in the box, continuous integration, microservices architecture, continuous deploy
Spectral Workbench	https://github.com/ publiclab/spectral-workbench	A web based application to collect, archive, share, and analyze spectral data, for public lab DIY spectrometers and other spectrometers	Continuous integration, legacy in the box, continuous testing, continuous deploy, microservices architecture
Salicml	https://github.com/ lappis-unb/salic-ml/	A web application that processed business indicators from cultural projects and presented them in a web dashboard to optimize the analysis of each project accountability by the technical team from the Brazilian Ministry of Culture	Continuous integration, continuous testing, continuous deploy

Table 3. Noosfero comparative: before DevOps and after DevOps.

Noosfero		
	Before DevOps	After DevOps
Docker/Docker compose	Misconfigured. Services were properly split but with several misconfigurations. Not used in production	Working properly for development and production environments
Framework version	Rails 4.2.4 with several deprecated dependencies and vendors. A lot of monkey-patches	Updated to Rails 5.1.6 with latest features
Continuous integration	GitLabCI builds took too long to finish and had important pipelines missing	Implemented caching to speed things up and added missing builds to the pipeline executor
Continuous deploy	None	None
Coding stylesheet	None. Every developer had its own technique	Configured a stylesheet and integrated it with the CI pipelines, and fixed all of the linting errors

6.1 Noosfero

Noosfero is a vast system, with over 70 database tables. Since there was a stable Continuous Integration tool set up and microservices have been widely made use of, there were only a couple of DevOps related improvements to do.

During the Noosfero study, which has been done first, there was a limited implementation for containers and continuous integration. Since it was the first upgrade of this kind that it has been worked on, a few errors have resulted in valuable learnings. When the Rails framework upgrade started, it was noticed that some steps should have been taken before, which would make the upgrade less painful.

In the middle of the refactoring, the Continuous Integration pipeline could have been improved by adding other testing stages, which could have identified some issues that appeared later. For instance, by previously adding a stage that tested out the Docker image building, we could assure every time that we included a change, this part of the project could remain stable. Also by including a code quality and stylesheet compliance stage we could also assure that our code refactoring was changing the code for the better, by making it more maintainable for example.

The project was also not properly wrapped in a container image, which should have been done before the upgrade started. By wrapping up the monolith through the concept of Legacy in the box, there was a homogeneous environment for every developer to work with. That has provided a consistent environment for the Noosfero application. In a different approach, Docker containers ensure consistency across multiple development and release cycles, thus standardizing the Noosfero environment.

Realistically, containerizing Noosfero before upgrading the Rails framework has been of great advantage; that meant parity, meaning that the Noosfero images ran the same no matter which server or whose laptop they were running on. The Noosfero study case only involved me as developer for this task, even though the maintainers allowed me to freely experiment the strategies, as in Mapknitter, due to the project complexity and few resources, by the end of the study it was possible to apply only the Legacy in the Box and Continuous Integration strategies.

It was also acknowledged that the Continuous Integration tool could be better used in terms of performance, so all of the testing and integration pipelines have been split to run in parallel since there was no inter-dependency between the suites. A style-sheet guide has also been added to this pipeline using Rubocop in order to enforce and obtain a more standardized code pattern (Table 4).

6.2 Mapknitter

The Mapknitter case study was a very challenging project. It includes various sub-components; among them, there is the core application written in Rails and a Javascript interface. At first, Docker has provided several benefits to the Mapknitter project itself but mostly for the Rails framework upgrade. The time required to build the container was very low, and in short time we had a working developing environment. During the containerization process, we could notice that the Travis CI tool had been using the production environment. So it was necessary to split the development, test and production environments, which has been done. With a few more improvements, Travis had set parallel jobs - what caused the builds to run twice as fast.

So by first adopting the concept of Legacy in the box, leads the update to take a further step and adopt the microservice architecture. That has been achieved at first, by splitting the MySQL database and the Mapknitter web app. Later

Table 4. Mapknitter comparative: Before DevOps and after DevOps.

Mapknitter		
	Before DevOps	After DevOps
Docker/Docker compose	Misconfigured. Database and services all wrapped in a container. Only worked in production	Working properly for development and production environments
Framework version	Deprecated Rails 3.2.2 with several deprecated dependencies	Updated to Rails 5.2.3 with latest features
Continuous integration	Misconfigured TravisCI, worked poorly	Improved to cached pipelines with reduced timeouts with more stages running in parallel
Continuous deploy	Misconfigured JenkinsCI, didn't work	Improved build and startup steps arrangement in order to have it working the best way it could. Every repository push would trigger a build that could be followed live.
Coding stylesheet	None. Despite the other Org repositories had it configured	Configured a stylesheet and integrated it with the CI pipelines, and fixed all of the linting errors. Thus, making the project following the org's coding patterns

we got also to containerize the ForeGo service, thus having three independent services running alongside.

Later on the project, we also got to setup Rubocop linter and stylesheet, which following the same standards used in Plots2 project - other project part of the PublicLab community ecosystem. By doing this, now there was a more cohesive and uniform set of projects in the organization. Also this linting tool has been integrated with the continuous integration tool to keep track of the syntax changes.

This refactoring involved two developers, me and another member of the community, the maintainers let us work very freely through the process, what has given us the chance to explore and try several ways of applying the strategies. And by the end of the Mapknitter study it was possible to apply a wide set of strategies, which were, in order: Legacy in the Box, Continuous Integration, Microservices architecture and Continuous Deploy (Table 5).

6.3   Spectral Workbench

In this case study I was more mature, so there was already an implicit order of strategies to be applied. First the docker workflow of the project was rewritten, since it was an "old" repository - with very legacy code and practices, it required some restructuring and refactoring on the configuration files. For instance, the MySQL instance was not dockerized and there was no automation that aided a developer to easily start coding.

Table 5. Spectral workbench comparative: Before DevOps and after DevOps.

Spectral workbench		
	Before DevOps	After DevOps
Docker/Docker compose	None	Working properly for development and production environments
Framework version	Rails 3.2.3 with several deprecated dependencies and vendors	Updated to Rails 5.2.4 with latest features
Continuous integration	Misconfigured TravisCI, worked poorly	Improved to cached pipelines with reduced timeouts with more stages running in parallel
Continuous deploy	None	Configured JenkinsCI pipelines. Build and startup steps arranged in order to have it working the best way it could. Every repository push would trigger a build that could be followed live
Coding stylesheet	None	Configured a stylesheet and integrated it with the CI pipelines, and fixed all of the linting errors

The Continuous Integration tool needed to be configured to execute local builds, so that we could obtain a testing environment that simulated faithfully both the development and production environment. This same CI tool previously was configured to run all tests at once - what caused the builds to take valuable coding time. So I had to split the test running by groups, in a way that each test suite was executed separately, thus taking advantage of the parallelism provided by the tool.

When it comes to testing, a main request of one of the maintainers was the configuration and inclusion of system tests and increase of the test coverage. Both of the requirements have been accomplished.

After the Rails framework upgrade was complete, it was required a staging environment so that we could test out the changes that were made on the cloud, a staging environment. So along with the help of PublicLab's sysadmin this was set, in an automated manner. And with Rubocop we got to standardize the coding style among the several contributors; the Rubocop settings used were the same as the ones used in Plots2, Mapknitter and Spectral Workbench.

The Spectral Workbench study case only involved me as developer, the maintainers let me work very freely through the process, what gave me the chance to explore and try new strategies, besides the ones I had used in previous study cases, via Continuous Testing. And by the end of the study it was possible to apply the greater set of strategies of all study cases: Continuous Integration,

Legacy in the Box, Continuous Testing, Continuous Deploy, Microservices architecture (Table 6).

6.4   Salicml

Table 6. Salicml Comparative: Before DevOps and after DevOps.

Salicml		
Docker/Docker compose	None	Working properly in development and production environments. Included a private database proxy to abstract VPN connections to developers. Multiple configurations to reflect every existing environment
Framework version	Django 2.2	Django 2.2
Continuous integration	None	Configured Gitlab CI tool to check on docker builds and automated test running. Integrated CI tool with docker containers management
Continuous deploy	None	Configured properly. Totally automated by using Rancher and Watchtower tools
Coding stylesheet	None	None

In the Salicml study I have not worked directly in this project, so that I could obtain a third-party point of view regarding the DevOps strategies to apply and their respective order of application. This different approach was very useful, as it helped reasserting certain practices applied in the previous studies, and thus it was possible forming them into strategies.

First it was included a docker development workflow for both development and production environments. A private database proxy to abstract VPN connections to developers was also included.

Also, the main application image was built from another custom image. In practice, whenever a change was inserted into the codebase and it didn't affect the application's dependencies, the requirements docker image didn't have to be rebuilt, thus optimizing the pipeline resources usage.

This refactoring involved Victor Moura, the maintainers allowed him to work very freely through the process, what has given him the change to use a wide set of tools. And by the end of the Salicml study it was possible to apply a great range of strategies, which were, in order: Legacy in the Box, Continuous Integration, Microservices architecture and Continuous Deploy. The main focus of this study in question was containerizing the legacy software and assure evolvalibility of it through the implementation of the Microservices architecture.

7 Discussion

One of the most important things that could be extracted from those refactorings is that the order of the strategies to apply matters a lot. For instance, if you choose to implement Continuous Deploy in your legacy software before having Continuous Integration set up, you could be taking a lot of risks by pushing certain amount of untested code to the cloud, or even be wasting a lot of precious time by manually testing it first and then deploying.

Considering another hypothetical case, one could choose to split the various components of the legacy software in several services - thus taking advantage of the Microservices architecture strategy - but it does that before implementing the Legacy in the Box technique. It may be very complicated to keep this architecture change flowing in a good pace without taking advantage of the various benefits that a legacy in box tool, such as Docker, could bring. Actually, making the refactoring way easier. In fact, it means that choosing the right order of strategies to be applied could prevent one from taking several extra hours, even days, of massive manual labor.

As the first strategy one should take to embrace DevOps in a legacy project is having a Continuous Integration pipeline set up. With that - along with a minimum test coverage - one can assure that the small pieces of code are still working, thus guaranteeing a more trustful code base. It is also noticeable that implementing CI strategy first will absorb the time a developer would take to run tests every time future integrations happened.

After having the work environment CI-friendly, the next step one should take is wrapping the legacy app in a container. Every configuration, third-party packages, and abstraction get to be explicitly defined in a container image, also being able to run anywhere basically.

Continuous Deploy and Testing are desired strategies, especially when it comes to testing, but needing to deploy and test are not a bottleneck - until a certain point, of course, and this affirmation also depends on the size, developers, and business rules that this legacy software goes by. If one has the chance and time to keep continuously testing the legacy code and implement an integration to ship at every successful CI tool build, then those are convenient strategies to adopt.

Moreover, implementing microservices is what one would call an utterly optional strategy because it takes a lot of time and effort to do it correctly. If it is not done right, you will only obtain a distributed monolith, with every said "micro" service executing heavy operations. Furthermore, once one has adopted the previous strategies, it is considerably less painful to implement it.

Based on the experiences acquired through the results achieved in this work, the strategies implementation order should be:

(1) Continuous Integration
(2) Legacy in the Box
(3) Continuous Testing
(4) Continuous Deploy
(5) Microservices architecture.

Continuous Testing is by far the broadest strategy, meaning that almost every legacy should adopt it when embracing the DevOps practices; it holds great significance for organizations using DevOps for the regular deployment of software into production. Continuous Testing in DevOps essentially interweaves testing efforts into all stages of designing, developing, and deploying the software. When it is adequately implemented, an organization can get a constant insight into the robustness of the latest software build and ensure speedy delivery of high-quality software.

When it comes to Continuous Integration, we can not say it is as "mandatory" as Continuous Testing. However, it certainly is beneficial, and, indeed, it will save a lot of the developers time. Of course, it could be painful at first for the team, and adapting a legacy software to such practices could be considerably expensive. Implementing a trustful CI pipeline could involve complétely change a software development culture, adapt the organization and workflow, automate the testing bulk, and even provide certain infrastructure. Nevertheless, in the long term, the benefits are countless.

By having each piece of code verified by an automated build, a team is allowed to develop cohesive software more rapidly. Leading to significantly reduced integration problems and quick error detection. The main goal of Continuous Integration is to provide rapid feedback so that if a *bug* is introduced into the codebase, it can be identified and corrected as soon as possible.

As in Continuous Integration, Continuous Deploy, when done right, is full of benefits, but implementing a trustful pipeline may be irksome as in CI. The technical parts are more comfortable than the organizational and cultural parts when it comes to legacy software. However, once this bottleneck is overcome, CD presents several benefits that directly influence the end product. Certainly, Continuous Deploy, when done right, is very fruitful - primarily when used along with Continuous Integration. Since failures are detected faster and fixed faster, it leads to higher release rates, making it possible to evaluate new code faster - and in smaller portions - thus allowing the developers to focus on the product features themselves.

Containerization, or commonly legacy in the box, is by far the strategy that presents one of the most significant benefits of all strategies. It is the fastest and straightforward strategy to implement. It does not require special technical knowledge and gives support to the other strategies. It is a common misconception that using containers only makes sense if the app to be hosted is composed of microservices, but monolithic deployments can benefit from containers. Using a container provider for the legacy code immediately makes it easy to move the app from one host to another just by migrating the previously generated container image. Every developer is using the same container image - this means consistency. Several other benefits intrinsically appear with the mentioned aspects, such as scalability, bare-metal access to the hardware, easy distributing, and much.

Two significant benefits are perceived by using containers as part of the Legacy in the Box strategy. First, resource utilization is much more efficient. Second, containers are cheap in man-hours to maintain and represent only a few costs a machine's resources. Container technology supports streamlined build, test, and deployment from the same container images; it enables Continuous Integration and Deploy. By using a container provider for the legacy code, one can immediately make it easy to move the app from one host to another just by migrating the previously generated container image.

Packaging the legacy code as a container, distributing it through an image repository is very facilitated. Anyone with access can pull the container image and run it. Every developer is using the same container image - this means consistency.

In legacy apps context, the meaning of the word containerization needs to be augmented to include all that is necessary to make an existing app ready to adopt Legacy in the Box concept. That is, to an extent that is well balanced with technical feasibility and expected business benefits. Choosing the right legacy containerization technique within this spectrum is a matter of striking the right balance between investment, business outcome, cost-effectiveness gain, technical feasibility, and risk appetite [4].

While this practice delivers some benefits, it does not offer the full benefits of modular, container-based application architecture. Using containerization to the fullest involves refactoring the existing applications to adapt to the containers thoroughly. That could quickly scale out, thus providing better support for microservices architecture. Container technology supports streamlined build, test, and deployment from the same container images; it means better support for Continuous Integration and Deploy.

At last, the Microservices strategy provides many advantages, but to the right contexts. One of the most significant advantages of a microservice over a monolithic architecture is that a microservice architecture allows different components to scale at different rates. The flexibility of microservices lets a system expand fast without requiring a significant increase in resources.

Also talking about the benefits of it, we have that, for instance, we know that every single microservice work independently and thus can be written with different technologies, and since all services are independent, developers are allowed to add, replace, and remove different services without influencing the already existent services.

Nevertheless, sometimes, using different languages, libraries, frameworks, and data storage technologies can be intimidating and paralyzing for organizations at first. They could become a "Frankenstein" of services that a long term. Plus, not every team can handle the autonomy, and independence microservices offer. Like any architectural approach, Microservices are hard to design correctly, and one should plan a lot before adopting this strategy.

Finally, one should consider these techniques or strategies just the plain basics the would start permitting the evolution and maintainability of a legacy code with DevOps. That means continuously and safely update the legacy project's dependencies, keep refactoring the code so that its quality enhaces - by following the SOLID and Clean Code premises, this refactoring should also get done in a way that leads to the componentization of the various parts of the code and when adding new features, assure that these are matching the current language standards.

It is also important to mention that throughout this entire automation process the very own team of the legacy project qualifies in DevOps technologies, thus adapting the development (Dev) and operations (Ops) processes and premisses according to the DevOps culture.

8   Conclusion

The theme that this work is filled with is very relevant to the software community. Having a guide on the most valuable software strategies is much needed. Having a personal analysis of someone who has already been through the experience of it, is even more relevant.

A realistic analysis of the DevOps strategies might help several teams that aim to modernize their much-cherished legacy systems. It could give them guidance to consider the upcoming steps to take and provide an overview of the importance of certain things.

Based on real-world experience, we set out the strategies, benefits, and countermeasures for each team with a specific condition or need. This work consisted of obtaining abstract information from previous experiences when upgrading legacy software. We have extracted data based on two of those experiences and mashed into the strategies that have been portrait in previous sections.

Of course, the DevOps culture of practices presents several other practices and mindsets to make beneficial strategies. However, the strategies presented here were considered more relevant, and the ones that present the most impact in outdated legacy software.

References

1. What is CI/CD? [n.d.]. https://www.redhat.com/en/topics/devops/what-is-ci-cd, Accessed Dec 2019
2. 6 Key Challenges of DevOps Implementation (2006). http://blog.vassit.co.uk/6-key-challenges-of-implementing-a-devops-strategy. Accessed Jan 2020
3. The Symbiotic Relationship of DevOps and Open Source (2016). https://techspective.net/2016/06/01/symbiotic-relationshipdevops-open-source/. Accessed Dec 2020
4. Containerization of legacy applications (2020). https://developer.ibm.com/technologies/containers/articles/containerization-of-legacyapplications/. Accessed Dec 2020
5. Open source leads to DevOps success (2020). https://techbeacon.com/devops/open-source-leads-devops-success. Accessed Dec 2020
6. The Way of DevOps: A Primer on DevOps Principles and Practices (2020). https://www.smartsheet.com/devops. Accessed Nov 2019
7. What is DevOp (2020). https://aws.amazon.com/devops/what-isdevops/?nc1=h_ls. Accessed Oct 2020
8. Balalaie, A., Heydarnoori, A., Jamshid, P.: An Experience Report on Migration to a Cloud-Native Architecture, Microservices Architecture Enables DevOps (2016)

9. Bogner, J., Fritzsch, J., Wagner, S., Zimmermann, A.: Assuring the evolvability of microservices: insights into industry practices and challenges. In: 019 IEEE International Conference on Software Maintenance and Evolution (ICSME), Cleveland, Ohio, USA (2014)
10. Wayne Cascio and Ramiro Montealegre. 2016. How Technology Is Changing Work and Organizations (2016)
11. Chiang, C.-C., Bayrak, C.: Legacy Software Modernization (2006)
12. Chima. R.: Legacy Software: How To Tell If Your Software Needs Replacing. https://www.bbconsult.co.uk/blog/legacy-software. Accessed Dec 2019
13. Noosfero Contributors. 2007. Noosfero. https://gitlab.com/noosfero/noosfero
14. Dobbert, M.L.: Ethnographic Research: Theory and Application for Modern Schools and Societies (Praeger Studies in Ethnographic Perspectives on American Education), 1st edn. Praeger (1 January 1982), Nova Southeastern University, Fort Lauderdale (2013)
15. Alex Edmonds, W., Kennedy, T.D.: An Applied Guide to Research Designs : Quantitative, Qualitative, and Mixed Methods, 2nd edn. SAGE Publications, Inc. (39 May 2016), Nova Southeastern University, Fort Lauderdale (2016)
16. Eeles. P.: What Is A Software Architecture? (2006)
17. Errickson-Connor, B.: Truth or Consequences (2003)
18. Fowler, M., Beck, K.: What Is Refactoring? In Refactoring: Improving the Design of Existing Code, vol. 1, p. 9. O'Reilly Media, Inc., Sebastopol (2002)
19. Garlan, D., Show, M.: An Interoduction to Software Architecture (1993)
20. Golden, B.: 3 reasons why you should always run microservices apps in containers (2019). https://techbeacon.com/app-devtesting/3-reasons-why-you-should-always-run-microservices-appscontainers, Accessed Dec 2019
21. Greenough, C., Worth, D.J.: The Transformation of Legacy Software: Some Tools and a Process (2003)
22. Saugatuck Technology Incorporated: Why DevOps Matters: Practical Insights on Managing Complex & Continuous Change (2014)
23. Khanam. Z.: Analyzing Refactoring Trends and Practices in the Software Industry (2018)
24. Leite, L., Rocha, C., Kon, F., Milojicic, D., Meirelles, P.: A Survey of DevOps Concepts and Challenges (2019)
25. Meyer, M.: Continuous Integration and Its Tools (2014)
26. Murphy, N.: Site Reliability Engineering Book, 1st edn. O'Reilly Media, Google Ireland (26 April 2016)
27. Namiot, D., Sneps-Sneppe, M.: On Micro-services Architecture (2014)
28. opensource.com. 2019: What is open source software? | Opensource.com. https://opensource.com/resources/what-open-source. Accessed Dec 2019
29. Rajlich, V.: Five Recommendations for Software Evolvability (2018)
30. Hari Rao, G.: Devops for Legacy Systems - The Demand of the Changing Applications Landscape (2018)
31. Rizvi, S.A.M. Khanam, Z.: A Methodology for Refactoring Legacy Code (2011)
32. Danilo Sato, Arif Wider, and Christoph Windheuser. 2019. Continuous Delivery for Machine Learning. (2019)
33. Singh, A., Bansal, R.K., Jha, N.: Open Source Software vs Proprietary Software (2015)
34. Smeds, J., Nybom, K., Porres, I.: A Definition and Perceived Adoption Impediments, DevOps (2015)
35. Sommerville, I.: Software Engineering, 10th edn., Pearson; Hoboken (24 March 2015)
36. Zhu, L., Bass, L., Champlin-Scharff, G.: DevOps and Its Practices (2016)

UX-Painter: Fostering UX Improvement in an Agile Setting

Juan Cruz Gardey[1,2(✉)], Julián Grigera[1,2,3], Gustavo Rossi[1,2],
and Alejandra Garrido[1,2]

[1] LIFIA, Fac. Informática, Univ. Nac. de La Plata, La Plata, Argentina
{jcgardey,juliang,gustavo,garrido}@lifia.info.unlp.edu.ar
[2] CONICET, La Plata, Argentina
[3] CIC-PBA, Pcia, La Plata, Argentina

Abstract. It is generally difficult in agile teams, specially those geographically distributed, to keep up with the user experience (UX) issues that emerge on each product increment. UX designers need the help of developers to set up user testing environments and to code improvements to the user interface, while developers are too busy with functionality issues. This paper describes a tool called UX-Painter and shows through a case study, how it may help in the above setting to synchronize UX practices and allow for continuous UX improvement during an agile development. UX-Painter allows designers to set up A/B testing environments, exploring interface design alternatives without the need of programming skills, through predefined transformations called client-side web refactorings. Once a design alternative is selected to be implemented in the application's codebase, UX-Painter may also facilitate this step, exporting the applied refactorings to different frontend frameworks. Thus, we foster a method where UX backlog items can be systematically tackled and resolved in an agile setting.

Keywords: Agile methods · User experience · Web engineering

1 Introduction

User Experience (UX) is crucial for the success of web applications. Adopting a User-Centered Design (UCD) approach ensures that software products are analyzed, designed and evaluated pursuing a high usability and UX, by allocating a significant amount of resources to user research [15]. However, UCD practices, as many research studies have pointed out, do not integrate well with agile methods [6,7,15]. While agile methods pursue customer satisfaction, UCD focuses on the user needs [6,15], but most importantly, UCD practices are too costly for agile teams, which usually cannot allot time for UX improvement during agile cycles. Recent methods, like Lean UX, aim at incorporating user research and Design Thinking practices into agile software development through a high degree of collaboration among UX designers and developers in a team [14]. Moreover, there are several artifacts being used to promote collaboration and communication

C. Rocha et al. (Eds.): WBMA 2021, CCIS 1642, pp. 54–65, 2023.
https://doi.org/10.1007/978-3-031-25648-6_4

among team members in the early phases of product design [10]. However, there is still a gap in practices and artifacts at late stages, when UX issues rise on already deployed product increments and UX improvement should take place, i.e., when solutions to UX issues should be evaluated, compared, communicated to developers and implemented [11].

In a previous work, we have developed UX-Painter, a visual programming tool for UX designers to set up alternative designs without the need of any script programming knowledge [11]. The building blocks to create alternative designs in UX-Painter are Client-Side Web Refactorings (CSWRs). A CSWR is a predefined transformation on a webpage element or interaction, which is intended to solve a specific UX issue while preserving the underlying functionality. UX-Painter allows designers to quickly set up new versions of a production web application by combining CSWRs. Thus, in an agile scenario where the UX of a product increment is evaluated at the end of a sprint and the issues found are incorporated in the next sprint backlog [9], UX designers may use UX-Painter to test alternative fixes to those issues while development of other backlog items proceeds.

The refactorings in UX-Painter are scripts that perform alterations on a rendered web page. The alterations are intended to improve the user interaction while preserving the underlying functionality [12]. An application version is created by applying and saving a set of refactorings. A version may be exported to be recreated on other browsers at the time of user testing.

Finally, once a particular version of the web application is selected after testing, it must be added to the product backlog for its implementation in the next sprint. However, in the context of time pressures imposed by agile development, UX-related backlog items are often left unattended to prioritize other backlog items such as bug fixes or new features. This context may lead to the accumulation of UX debt [4]. The UX debt metaphor refers to a degraded UX quality caused by shortcuts taken to speed up development and that becomes a burden for agile teams to maintain. Having a large amount of UX debt can negatively impact the users, affecting the application success.

Thus, the proposal in this work is to use UX-Painter once again, but this time to help developers in the process of implementing the new version of the application in the code base. For this purpose we have extended UX-Painter to generate the code required by each and every CSWR in the selected application version, for the libraries and frameworks used nowadays to build web user interfaces [19]. Developers then may adapt this source code to fit it in the target application instead of having to code the solutions from scratch. We believe that using the generated code as a baseline can help developers to reduce the refactorings implementation effort, which in turn will allow to give more priority to UX-related items as they become easier to solve.

Summarizing, the contribution of this work is an artifact that facilitates the integration of UCD and agile methods, helping both roles involved in UX improvement. On the one hand, UX-Painter helps UX designers to quickly explore alternative designs. On the other hand, UX-Painter assists developers when they have to code those design changes evaluated by UX designers. Our case study that uses the ReactJS framework shows that the generated code reduced refactorings implementation effort.

The paper is organized as follows. Next section describes some related work. Section 3 describes how the UX improvement can be introduced in an agile process. Section 4 shows UX-Painter in action with a concrete example, and Sect. 5 presents an extension which allows exporting the applied CSWRs to ReactJS[1], one of the most popular front-end libraries. We finish with a conclusion and future work.

2   Related Work

The values and principles of agile methods make them quite appropriate to involve users in the development process. Thus, incorporating UX aspects is an issue that both the academy and industry have studied for years [6]. Studies involving practitioners, like the one presented by Larusdottir et al. [16] show that incorporating UX aspects in agile projects is difficult in practice, and UX professionals need a more prominent role in the team. Many authors have indicated the lack of support for including and tracing UX requirements in a systematic and coordinated way [2,7]. In a recent study on an agile team in UK, Zaina et al. [21] found many problems in the UX information flow, such as user perspective aspects not being captured with artifacts, but rather verbally.

To bridge the gap between developers and UX designers in the team, prototyping has been widely used as an effective communication device among team members and with end users [14]. Different approaches emerged to tackle UX requirements in agile cycles with the help of prototyping, like UXUF-AP [18] that proposes the use of prototypes along with UX and Usability guidelines. Modern applications like Figma or InVision allow creating high fidelity prototoypes containing basic interactions, being an effective way to get a feel of the final product. Similar tools have also been proposed by research groups, like Poirot [20], to enable designers make style edits to websites, in a similar fashion of browser developer tools, but with a heavier focus on UI design rather than code edition. However, they do not support making quick changes to already deployed user interfaces (UIs).

Different research works have tackled the need for applying quick alterations to running UIs. The field of web augmentation proposes alterations to be applied on the client-side, even of third party applications, for specific viewpoints or contexts [1]. For example, Ghiani et al. [13] use web augmentation to adapt the UI to different contexts of use (technology, users or environment). Other approaches propose empowering end-users, allowing them to create personalized contents such as WebMakeUp [8]. Our work can be considered as web augmentation proposal that, rather than personalizing content or adapting an interface to different contexts, has the focus on improving the UX.

---

[1]   https://reactjs.org.

Another approach worth mentioning is the technique of generating code from raster images. There are studies that analyze how to facilitate UI development, like the work of Bajammal et al. [3], or pix2code [5], which constitutes a good alternative for materializing quickly drafted prototypes. The difference with our approach is that they focus on deriving the code of the complete UI from mock-ups, which is useful at early stages, but not for incremental adjustments required to fix UX problems at later stages. There are however tool-supported approaches that consider code generation from prototypes in later development stages over already deployed UIs [17], but they use computer vision over annotated proto-types, which involves an additional step.

3   A UX-Aware Agile Process

The use of digital artifacts is one of the key factors to achieve an integration between the agile and UX worlds [6,7]. While their importance is clear, there is a lack of artifacts used for communication between developers and designers, specially when there already is a developed UI and it should be improved for a better UX.

For that purpose, we propose UX-Painter to mediate collaboration between developers and designers in two main stages of a UX-aware agile process (see Fig. 1). One stage is when designers need to explore alternative designs as solutions to UX problems found in the previous product increment, so they can do it on their own without requiring developers' assistance in setting up testing environments. The second stage is when developers need to implement the selected solutions in the next product increment. Figure 1 depicts an agile process (middle section) and the two stages where UX-Painter may participate: the first stage is shown in blue in the upper side of the figure, and the second stage is shown in orange in the lower side. The figure identifies three main activities in each sprint: a *sprint planning*, in which the team selects from the product backlog the features to be implemented in the sprint; the *sprint execution*, when the team starts working on the selected features; and the *sprint review*, which is the meeting at the end of the sprint intended to inspect and evaluate the product increment built during the sprint.

In the process that we propose, the sprint review may be used to show the product increment (PI) to the client and perform functionality testing as well as user testing to evaluate UX [9]. During the next sprint planning, the discovered UX issues may be incorporated in the sprint backlog to be handled by UX designers. Then, during the sprint execution, designers may use UX-Painter to explore design alternatives to fix the UX issues, creating new versions of the PI. Thus, they can dispense developers from coding these new versions, and developers instead can focus on adding or fixing functionality issues from the product backlog. Moreover, designers may plan and execute new user tests of the alternative versions generated with UX-Painter, to assess which one of them works best.

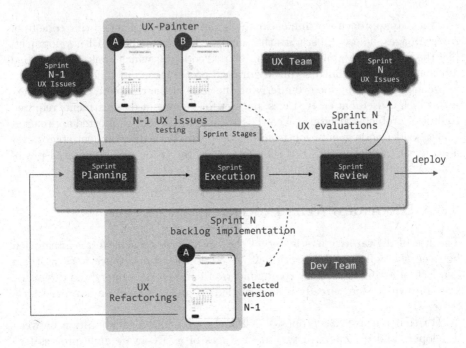

Fig. 1. UX-Painter in an agile setting.

In this way, developers only participate in the UX improvement process when they have to implement design changes (in terms of refactorings) that have been tested. According to the process shown, these changes will be available in the next sprint to be selected for implementation. Then, at the sprint planing of the next iteration, developers can divide their work between solving the previous UX issues and the rest of product backlog items, like new features or bug fixing. When solving UX issues, developers can use the code generated by UX-Painter to make the implementation of refactorings faster. Finally, in the review meeting at the end of the sprint, the process starts again with designers conducting user tests on the new PI and finding the new UX issues, which will be tackled in the next sprint.

Reducing the time required to test alternative designs and to implement them, can help both designers and developers to pay more attention to the UX improvement that is important to keep the UX-debt under control, but without losing the focus on adding new functionality, which is crucial in an agile setting.

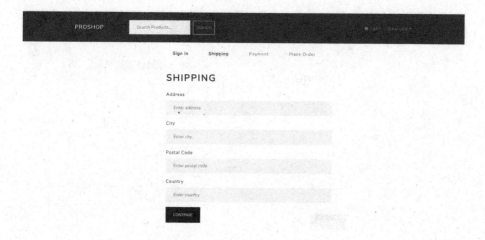

Fig. 2. Checkout form of an e-commerce web application

4 UX-Painter in Action

UX-Painter is a web-extension that allows creating alternative designs of a web application by applying small transformations through the assisted application of Client-Side Web Refactorings (CSWRs). The alternative designs generated can then be saved as application's versions for further evaluations such as A/B testing or inspection reviews [11]. To show a concrete example of the tool usage, suppose that a team is working on an e-commerce web application[2]. In the previous sprint, developers worked on the checkout process, building the UI shown in Fig. 2. The UX team decided to use UX-Painter to inspect some design changes. For example, the shipping form does not provide a client validation. Even when the user submits the form without filling in any field, the information is sent to the server for its validation. In order to minimize failed form submissions because of incomplete information, a prior validation can be added to check mandatory fields. The CSWR that includes this feature is *Add Late Form Validation*.

The changes are made on a specific version, so the first step to apply a refactoring is to create a new application's version (see Fig. 3). When the new version is edited, all the available CSWRs are listed. Once a refactoring is selected, the tool guides the user through the process of applying it. This process is similar for all the refactorings: the user selects the target element to be refactored directly over the target page, then fills in refactoring-specific parameters (*Add Late Form Validation* requires the fields to be checked when the form is submitted) and finally confirms the changes after observing a preview. For instance, in *Add Late Form Validation*, the preview shows that when the submit button is clicked, a red border is added to the mandatory empty fields.

---

[2] https://github.com/bradtraversy/proshop_mern.

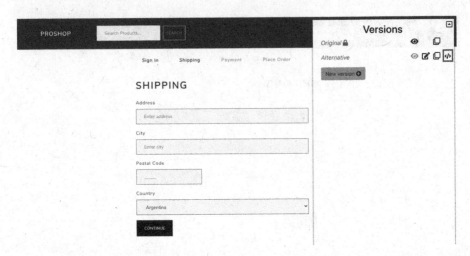

Fig. 3. Alternative version of the shipping form with some refactorings applied. The "eye" icons allow to show the target version.

UX-Painter gives the possibility to combine different refactorings to produce larger design changes. In the form previously refactored, another UX issue is in the country field. Given that it expects a value from a predefined list, using a free text input to enter the value can be error-prone. In order to facilitate the input, the country field can be replaced with a select box including predefined options by applying *Turn Input into Select.* For this refactoring, the user must provide the option list that will be displayed in the select box.

Postal code field can also be changed to improve the user interaction. In particular, assuming that postal codes have only numbers and at most 5 digits, a mask can be applied through the refactoring *Format Input*, to prevent the format errors that may arise. Moreover, through *Resize Input* the field can be narrowed to give the users a hint of the expected input length. The new version of the shipping form is shown in Fig. 3, besides UX-Painter's versions menu. It can be observed that although the user interface suffered different modifications, the underlying functionality was not altered, in the sense that a user is capable of performing the same set of operations as in the original version.

The designer must save the version with all the applied CSWRs to persist the changes. The tool saves in the browser's local storage the information needed to recreate each CSWR in future page's visits. A version can contain refactorings in different application pages. Anytime, the designer can choose which version to see to compare the differences. Whenever an application page is loaded, the tool executes all the refactorings belonging to the selected version that were applied on the target URL.

The next step for the UX team is to assess if the new version generated really causes an improvement for final users. The evaluation is important because it could happen that a refactoring does not improve significantly the user interaction on a specific application, or even the original UI can work better than the refactored one. Moreover, there are alternative refactorings that serve the same purpose, like *Add Datepicker* and *Date Input into Selects* that provide different ways to enter a date. In this case, the best refactoring for each particular situation depends on the context of use, so the different alternatives should be evaluated to find the right solution. To this end, designers can use UX-Painter to run user test sessions with some subjects to analyze how they interact with the different application versions. Finally, if the new version works better than the previous one, the UX team has to communicate the changes to developers to be implemented in the application's codebase during the following product increment. At this point, generating a preliminary version of the refactorings' source code can help developers to reduce the effort required for the implementation.

The next section describes the CSWR's code generation.

5   Implementing Refactorings

Following with the case study described in the previous section, this section shows the implementation of the refactorings applied in Fig. 3. Using UX-Painter it is possible to automatically generate a basic implementation of the refactorings for ReactJS (used in the application's front-end) that developers might adapt or refine when the evaluted UX issues have to be implemented on the application's codebase. Since each refactoring performs a very specific change, the differences between multiple instances of the same refactoring are on the parameters defined by the user who performs them. Therefore, it is possible to develop a template code for each refactoring that then can be completed with the parameters corresponding to a particular refactoring application.

In order to generate the code for a specific application version, the user must click on the "source-code" icon (highlighted with a red box in the top right of Fig. 3). Next, the tool shows a list of the generated ReactJS components. Components are the building blocks of a ReactJS application; they are basically JavaScript functions that define reusable pieces of the user-interface. For the version described in the previous section, Fig. 4 shows that there is only one component that contains the implementation for the whole shipping form. Since there are CSWRs that apply very small changes, it may not be realistic to create a different component for each refactoring. Instead, the tool looks for high-level elements that were refactored like a form, and creates one component with all the refactorings included in them. The generated source code for each refactoring appears in Fig. 5.

The source code generation process for a refactoring (or a group of refactorings that modify the same DOM element) begins with creating a very basic component consisting of the HTML code obtained from the refactored DOM node. In our case study, the target node is the form element that contains all the applied refactorings. Later, UX-Painter refines and augments this implementation according to the specifications of ReactJS and the changes that each refactoring performs. For example, in the case of *Add Late Form Validation*, a

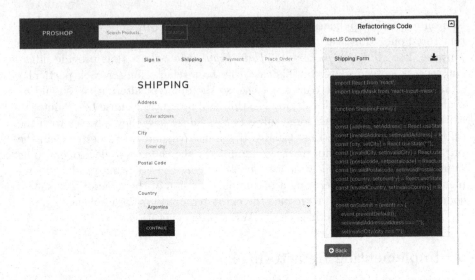

Fig. 4. ReactJS component generated for the alternative version. The user can observe a preview before downloading it.

boolean state is added for each mandatory field, to control whether the field is valid or not, and it is updated in the onSubmit event handler. This state is also used to highlight an invalid field by adding a red border to it. Concerning the implementation of the others refactorings, the tool replaces existing nodes and modifies their attributes. While *Turn Input into Select* substitutes the text input with the native select element including the corresponding options, *Format Input* replaces the input field by a component imported from a third-party library which encapsulates a text input with the logic of a mask.

Once the generated code is downloaded, it should be manually integrated with the application's codebase. This process depends on different factors of the codebase such as how the UI is divided into different components, the dependencies used, among others. Moreover, developers may need to extend the generated implementation. For instance, the countries displayed in the select box probably will be retrieved from an API instead of listing the options one by one, so the API request must be integrated in the generated component. Another example of a possible extension is in the fields validation. The refactoring *Add Late Form Validation* only validates that the fields are not sent empty to the server, but other validations like input formats compliance may also be required.

Thus, the goal of UX-Painter is not to give a full implementation of the CSWRs to paste directly in the codebase, but to provide a potential solution that developers can use as a starting point to integrate these refactorings into the target application. By observing the provided implementation, developers can at least understand how the refactorings work under the hood, and to get the HTML and CSS code modified by each refactoring.

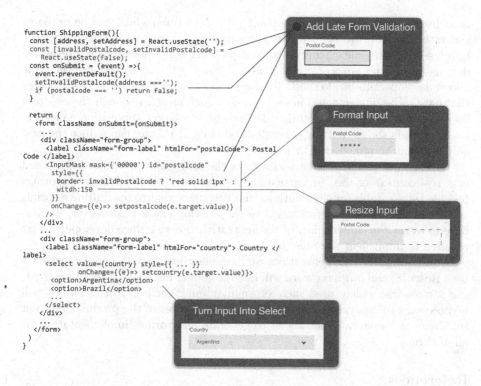

```
function ShippingForm(){
  const [address, setAddress] = React.useState('');
  const [invalidPostalcode, setInvalidPostalcode] =
    React.useState(false);
  const onSubmit = (event) =>{
    event.preventDefault();
    setInvalidPostalcode(address ==='');
    if (postalcode === '') return false;
  }

  return (
    <form className onSubmit={onSubmit}>
      ...
      <div className="form-group">
        <label className="form-label" htmlFor="postalCode"> Postal
Code </label>
        <InputMask mask={'00000'} id="postalcode"
          style={{
            border: invalidPostalcode ? 'red solid 1px' : '',
            witdh:150
          }}
          onChange={(e)=> setpostalcode(e.target.value)}
        />
      </div>
      ...
      <div className="form-group">
        <label className="form-label" htmlFor="country"> Country </
label>
        <select value={country} style={{ ... }}
            onChange={(e)=> setcountry(e.target.value)}>
          <option>Argentina</option>
          <option>Brazil</option>
          ...
        </select>
      </div>
      ...
    </form>
  )
}
```

Fig. 5. Code generated by UX-Painter. Changes imposed by each refactoring are highlighted and marked.

The results of using UX-Painter to generate the refactored code were quite promising, as code integration was straightforward. The structure of the generated component for the shipping form is similar to that of the codebase, which can be observed in the GitHub repository. We decided to use a third-party web application to avoid any bias of coding the case study ourselves.

Further experiments are necessary, as these results are limited to a single case study, and the selected application is small-sized (so the code could fit in the available space). Although other cases may show that the refactored code offered by UX-Painter is not entirely suitable or difficult to integrate, we believe that the tool is helpful for both designers and developers, for experimenting with ready-to-apply solutions to UX problems, for communicating this solutions to the whole team, and to provide at least good hints of how to code them.

6   Conclusion

This paper described UX-Painter, a tool that allows synchronizing and communicating UX practices, fostering a method for the systematic improvement of UX issues. This is especially relevant in the context of in agile cycles, since they focus on delivering new functionality in short periods of time, which can be prone to generate UX debt. We believe that the nature of UX-painter makes it particularly useful in an agile setting because it provides support to set up alternative designs for testing purposes, and it also facilitates their implementation. This allows developers to tackle the UX issues without leaving aside the new features that have to be implemented in each product increment. Although the concrete implementation of each refactoring depends on the target application codebase, our case study shows that the generated code by UX-Painter can reduce the load on developers to remediate UX issues.

Future work includes the assessment of the tool with the workflow proposed in a real context of use. In particular, we plan to evaluate if the refactorings provided are suitable for the solutions that designers want to test during a sprint, and to incorporate new refactorings to the existing catalog. Moreover, we also have to assess the effectiveness of the generated code to reduce developers effort required to implement the refactorings.

Concerning the code generation, we have described here the implementation with ReactJS, and our next work will include adding full support for other front-end frameworks widely used such as Angular[3] and Vue.js[4]. To this end, it will be necessary to analyze the similarities and differences of the products in order to develop a framework that allows to generate refactorings implementation for all of them.

References

1. Aldalur, I., Winckler, M., Díaz, O., Palanque, P.: Web augmentation as a promising technology for end user development. In: Paternò, F., Wulf, V. (eds.) New Perspectives in End-User Development, pp. 433–459. Springer, Cham (2017). https://doi.org/10.1007/978-3-319-60291-2_17

2. Almughram, O., Alyahya, S.: Coordination support for integrating user centered design in distributed agile projects. In: 15th IEEE/ACIS International Conference on Software Engineering Research, Management and Applications, pp. 229–238 (2017)

3. Bajammal, M., Mazinanian, D., Mesbah, A.: Generating reusable web components from mockups. In: Proceedings of the 33rd ACM/IEEE International Conference on Automated Software Engineering, ASE 2018, pp. 601–611 (2018)

4. Baltes, S., Dashuber, V.: UX debt: developers borrow while users pay (2021). https://arxiv.org/abs/2104.06908

5. Beltramelli, T.: pix2code: generating code from a graphical user interface screenshot. In: Proceedings of the ACM SIGCHI Symposium on Engineering Interactive Computing Systems, pp. 1–6 (2018)

6. Brhel, M., Meth, H., Maedche, A., Werder, K.: Exploring principles of user-centered agile software development: a literature review. Inf. Softw. Technol. **61**, 163–181 (2015)

7. Da Silva, T.S., Silveira, M.S., Maurer, F., Silveira, F.F.: The evolution of agile UXD. Inf. Softw. Technol. **102**, 1–5 (2018)

---

[3] https://angular.io.
[4] https://vuejs.org.

8. Díaz, O., Aldalur, I., Arellano, C., Medina, H., Firmenich, S.: Web mashups with WebMakeup. In: Daniel, F., Pautasso, C. (eds.) RMC 2015. CCIS, vol. 591, pp. 82–97. Springer, Cham (2016). https://doi.org/10.1007/978-3-319-28727-0_6
9. Firmenich, S., Garrido, A., Grigera, J., Rivero, J.M., Rossi, G.: Usability improvement through A/B testing and refactoring. Software Qual. J. **27**(1), 203–240 (2019)
10. Garcia, A., da Silva, T.S., Silveira, M.S.: Artifact-facilitated communication in agile user-centered design. In: Kruchten, P., Fraser, S., Coallier, F. (eds.) XP 2019. LNBIP, vol. 355, pp. 102–118. Springer, Cham (2019). https://doi.org/10.1007/978-3-030-19034-7_7
11. Gardey, J.C., Garrido, A., Firmenich, S., Grigera, J., Rossi, G.: UX-painter: an approach to explore interaction fixes in the browser. Proc. ACM Hum. Comput. Interact. **4**(EICS) (2020)
12. Garrido, A., Rossi, G., Distante, D.: Refactoring for usability in web applications. IEEE Softw. **28**(3), 60–67 (2011)
13. Ghiani, G., Manca, M., O, F.P.: Personalization of context-dependent applications through trigger-action rules. In: ACM TOCHI. vol. 24 (2017)
14. Gothelf, J., Seiden, J.: Lean UX: Designing Great Products with Agile Teams. O'Reilly Media, Inc. (2016)
15. Jurca, G., Hellmann, T.D., Maurer, F.: Integrating agile and user-centered design: a systematic mapping and review of evaluation and validation studies of agile-UX. In: Proceedings - 2014 Agile Conference, pp. 24–32 (2014)
16. Larusdottir, M., Gulliksen, J., Cajander, Å.: A license to kill-improving UCSD in agile development. J. Syst. Softw. **123**, 214–222 (2017)
17. Moran, K., Bernal-Cárdenas, C., Curcio, M., Bonett, R., Poshyvanyk, D.: Machine learning-based prototyping of graphical user interfaces for mobile apps. IEEE Trans. Softw. Eng. **46**(2), 196–221 (2018)
18. de Oliveira Sousa, A., Valentim, N.M.C.: Prototyping usability and user experience: a simple technique to agile teams. In: Proceedings of the XVIII Brazilian Symposium on Software Quality, pp. 222–227 (2019)
19. stateofjs: Worldwide usage of javascript front-end libraries. (2021). https://2021.stateofjs.com/en-US/libraries/front-end-frameworks
20. Tanner, K., Johnson, N., Landay, J.A.: Poirot: a web inspector for designers. In: Proceedings of the 2019 CHI Conference on Human Factors in Computing Systems, pp. 1–12 (2019)
21. Zaina, L., Sharp, H., Barroca, L.: UX information in the daily work of an agile team: a distributed cognition analysis. Int. J. Hum. Comput. Stud. **147** (2021)

Applying Agile Management on Communities of Practice and Startups: A Survey

Daniel Lima and Rodrigo Cursino[(⊠)]

CESAR School, Recife, Pernambuco, Brazil
{dnl,rbc}@cesar.school

Abstract. The work in communities has been expanding since the ascensus of technology-based companies, today called startups. Whether created informally or having a supporting company behind, it's hard to find any company that does not have at least a internal discussion group on the topic or support external initiatives related to topics and practices of interest. Today, events, formal and exclusive groups and meetups exist within this collaborative environment. This work aims to understand the motivations that these communities have to adopt Agile Methods in their management and how beneficial this can become for the management of knowledge transfer. 68 respondents stated that safe learning environments make the best positioned companies in their ecosystems and allow that new products are developed in a more collaborative way, even if unofficially, it can generate financial savings and learnings journeys.

Keywords: Agile management · Communities of practice · Communities of startups · Project management

1 Introduction

A community of practice (CoP) is a group of people who share a common concern, a set of problems, an interest in a topic, or a passion for something they do. They learn together how to do fulfill both individual and group goals and they interact regularly [1].

The emergence of startup communities in Brazil often takes place through connections created during events and meetups [2]. One example is the Startup Weekend[1], by Techstars. In Brazil, this event is quite traditional and have already had several editions. Another example of a community is Manguezal[2] which brings together professionals from several startups of Porto Digital[3], one of the largest technology and innovation parks in Brazil.

In some entrepreneurial communities, the target audience must always be more than 50% of the presence in activities and events. Feld et al. say if in a

---

[1] https://www.techstars.com/communities/startup-weekend.
[2] https://manguez.al/.
[3] https://www.portodigital.org/.

© Springer Nature Switzerland AG 2023
C. Rocha et al. (Eds.): WBMA 2021, CCIS 1642, pp. 66–78, 2023.
https://doi.org/10.1007/978-3-031-25648-6_5

startup community, for example, the presence of entrepreneurs is lower than 50% of the audience at an event or lecture, there is a fundamental problem, since the audience to whom he addresses his speech is not present. The same applies to communities of practice and business [3]. Also for you building a community of practice is necessary to articulate its values and identify suitable people to represent such values [1]. Regardless of the type of community, whenever someone new member joins, the community itself acts as a support network, aggregating the new members to their culture and their purpose [1]. Based on the principles of the Agile Manifesto, we can reinforce that communities of practices and startups seek to structure themselves through self-organizing teams that work in a collaborative way throughout the project [1, 4].

As much as the Manifesto for Agile Software Development defines that the interactions between the individuals involved in a software project should be more important than processes and tools, it does not exclude the need to have them used in a structured way [4]. Correlate the principles of the Agile Manifesto with the practices and needs of consultative groups, communities and events of innovation, entrepreneurship and technology are becoming common, given its easy applicability and also the number of members that uses such agile methods and practices in their work teams [5].

However, despite understanding the benefits of agile methods and learning processes, cases and existing collaborations in startup communities and practices Brazilian companies, we understand that there is room to connect more substantially the use of agile methodologies in the management of these initiatives.

So, the purpose of this work is to understand which agile methodologies and practices are used in the management or activities of communities of practice and startups. Also, we want to understand what are the objectives and benefits that organizations aim when creating and managing communities.

This work is organized based on the following structure: Sect. 2 presents the related works; the Research Method is presented in Sect. 3; Sect. 4 details the Results of the research; and the conclusion and future works are detailed in Sect. 5.

2   Related Works

Although there are several articles and scientific studies on Communities of Practices, many of them focus on knowledge management [6]. When we talk about Startup communities, there are several classic issues for continuity and longevity of organic communities such as these, including the commitment that should be in long term, but ends up becoming something to fill vacant spaces in the daily lives of entrepreneurs [3].

Feld et al., in their PhD Thesis, says that the commitment of entrepreneurs, who are part of Startup Communities, should be based in a long-term (in an average of 20 years, for example), respecting their limits and moments of life within ecosystems [3].

Emily Weber, on the other hand, says that in companies, employees have the desire for connecting with other people, throughout life and career, besides the need to be connected or supported by others [1]. Communities of practices can identify their members' soft skills and thus act as part of the personal development of the people involved there.

Considering communities that are under the corporate seal of some organization, Jono Bacon states in his work that hiring a professional community management team is essential to its success [7].

This team needs to be integrated with the company's goals and needs to have a solid training. Usually teams split up into three groups: community directors, managers of communities (Community Managers) and community evangelists (Community Evangelists). And all these people need to have specific domains in certain areas that the community is focused on discussing; be a kind person who generates empathy between people, becoming a focal point, especially for those who are arriving; and willing to grow, aligning strategies and leadership for rapid changes that may arise throughout the journey.

Borzillo et al. have as research objective to provide managers, researchers and consultants insights regarding the ways in which CoPs can support the refinements of products, discovery of new ones and the creation of learning spaces, so that the organizations can improve the adoption of agile practices and perform collaboration [8].

Finally, Kalenda et al. relate communities of practice as practice commonly applied when organizations want to adopt agility at scale. CoPs help in actions such as knowledge sharing and promotion of best practices on tools and processes among agile teams. Furthermore, they can also be used for coaching, coordination and continuous improvement processes [9].

3   Research Method

Survey is a research method that aims to gather data from a population of interest. Despite being widely used in software engineering, Survey-based research faces several challenges [10]. In this sense, this research is supported by the guideline for conducting surveys in software engineering proposed by J. Linåker et al. [11].

The objective of this research is to understand which agile methodologies and practices are used in the management or activities of communities of practice and startups. In addition, this study seeks to understand what are the objectives and benefits that organizations aim when creating and managing communities.

3.1   Research Questions

To fulfill the general objective, we formulate the following research questions:

- **RQ01**: What agile methods and practices are being used in management and operation of communities?
- **RQ02**: What are the main objectives of the companies and the aimed benefits when adopting communities?

3.2   Target Audience

As this study is related to communities, the target audience considered to understand their practices and needs, is based by entrepreneurs, employees of information technology companies, students in the fields of technology, business schools and people who are part of innovation ecosystems.

It is possible to observe in Table 1 the list of the types of communities and the main roles that the target audience of this research can play. Also, we also considered investors, startup programs managers, innovation parks and corporate ventures, spread across the Brazilian innovation ecosystems.

Table 1. Types of communities and roles of target audience.

Type of Communities	Roles in communities
- Startup communities - Communities of practice - Business communities	- Leadership - Regular member - Guest member - Support - consultant - Mentor - Investor

3.3   Research Tool

An online questionnaire with a total of 30 questions was implemented for data collection. They were distributed into the following groups: (i) demographic, (ii) agile methods and (iii) community management. A summary of the questions can be seen in Table 2.

The first set of questions is related to demographic data about the participants, their organizations/companies and from which communities they participate. We aim to understand how people develop new learning by joining the communities activities and events and sharing good practices into their organizations. Also, how their roles as members or leaders, for example, interfere in the management of communities and their longevity.

In the second group of questions, we want to understand the degree of knowledge of the participants about agile methods and practices and how they adopt them within the management activities of communities and their impact on the ecosystems that are involved.

Finally, the last set of questions seeks to know what the goals and benefits are found in the management of different types of communities: practice, startups or business.

The survey has a mix of open and closed questions. For closed ones were developed single-choice (SC) responses or multiple choice (MC) responses. For questions with multiple choice answers, the option "others" has been added.

Table 2. Summary view of the questionnaire.

Group	Id	Question	Type
Demographic	Q01	What's your name?	Open (optional)
	Q02	What's your email? ?	Open (optional)
	...	...	...
	Q08	Do you act or are part of a community (startups, practices, business...)?	Closed (SC)
	Q07	What is the size of the company do you work for?	Closed (MC)
	Q08.1	How long have you been working in the community(s)?	Closed (SC)
	Q08.2	What types of community(s) do you operate in?	Closed (MC)
	Q08.3	What is your role in the community(ies)?	Closed (MC)
Agile methods	Q09	How long have you been working with methodologies agile?	Closed (SC)
	Q10	How do you see the adoption of agile methodologies in your company?	Closed (SC)
	Q10.1	In your opinion, what are the benefits found in companies that adopt or encourage the creation of communities?	Open
	...	...	...
	Q12.2	What agile practices do you use or have used in your company?	Open
	Q12.3	What agile practices do you use or have used?	Closed (MC)
Community management	Q13	How does your company handle knowledge sharing?	Closed (MC)
	...	...	...
	Q15	What management methodology/practice have you used/used?	Closed (MC)
	Q16	Have you applied any management practices in your community(ies)?	Open
	...	...	...
	Q18	In your opinion, what is the importance of using agile methods in community management?	Likert scale
	Q19	What agile methods have you used within the community(ies)?	Closed (MC)
	...	...	...
	Q21	Which of these characteristics, in your opinion, define well the role of the community within a company?	Closed (MC)

Thus, respondents can enter specific answers, not listed above. In question 18 we used the Importance Level Likert Scale: 1 - not important; 2 - maybe it is important; 3 - it is important; 4 - is very important. For open questions, respondents can enter their responses in their own words, without the need of a standard. Questions 01 and 02 seek to capture name and e-mail and they are not mandatory.

3.4 Data Collection

This study used accidental sampling [11]. This means that the criterion of selection of samples is convenience. In this case, the researchers recruited participants of their professional connections and networking.

Each researcher set up a list of invitations with contacts from different companies and projects that use agile methodologies and have connection with communities. Another criterion used to make these lists was selecting people from different regions, so that we could have representatives from all over Brazil.

In addition, the survey was disseminated and shared in groups from some communities and also through some social networks like LinkedIn and Twitter.

The data collection phase took place between 8/17/2020 and 9/23/2020. The tool used for sending the research form, collecting and analyzing the data was Google Forms[4].

4   Results

In the following subsections, we summarize the results obtained from the application of the online survey based on the research questions. Furthermore, in the Subsect. 4.1 we present the results related to the demography of participants, including age and type of company.

4.1 Demographic Data

62 participants completed the responses on the submitted survey. They represent States of the 5 regions of Brazil, as shown in Fig. 1, with 63,2% respondents from states in the Northeast region, 14,3% from Southeast, 8,1% from South, 8% from the North and 6,4% from the Midwest region.

In Figs. 2(a) and 2(b) we can see that most respondents are cis men (51%) aged between 25 and 44 years (69,4%). Answers denote that the participation over 45 years old, who participate in communities of practices, startups and entrepreneurship is still very small, no adding a fifth of respondents. This is notable in events and gatherings face-to-face. Communities can be an excellent gateways to this new universe, since they are open to the point of attracting public with this age group.

Regarding the size of the companies they work for, based on the quantity of employees, it is possible to observe that the massive majority of respondents

---

[4] https://www.google.com/intl/pt-BR/forms/about/.

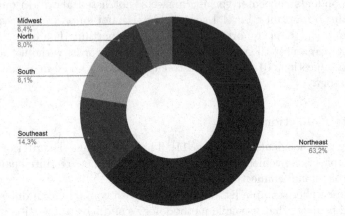

Fig. 1. Distribution of participants by regions of Brazil.

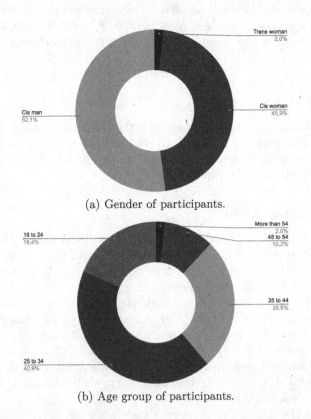

(a) Gender of participants.

(b) Age group of participants.

Fig. 2. Distribution of participants by gender and age group.

works in small or micro companies (76.6%), having up to 49 employees. 17% of respondents work in companies with up to 99 employees and the others (6.4%) in organizations with more than 100 employees.

4.2 RQ01: What Agile Methods and Practices are Being Used in Management and Operation of Communities?

Respondents needed to inform about their experience with the use of Agile Methodologies and all (100%) said they already use them, or used them in some time in your professional life. However, only 11.1% said that at the moment they are not working in any company or project based on over Agile Methods. 33.3% of respondents reported that their company adopts agility in its management, not limited to projects.

In addition, as we can see in Fig. 3, respondents assess that they are very important (62.5%) or important (25%) the use of agile methodologies for the community management. Only 6.3% understand that maybe it's not important and another 6.3% understand that agile methods do not influence the activity of management.

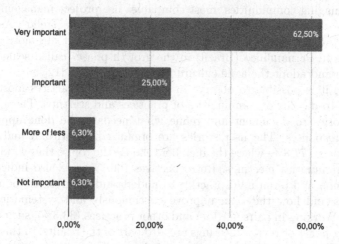

Fig. 3. Importance of the use of agile methods in community management.

When asked about agile methods used in managing communities (Fig. 4), we had Scrum and Kanban as the most indicated with 66.7% and 56.3%, respectively. These results are consistent and aligned with the result of the State of Agile Report that points out that the methods most popular agile methods applied in projects, consultancies and communities are the Scrum and Kanban or hybrid applications of these methodologies [5]. Lean was also cited having 33.3% of responses. 25% of respondents say they never have made use of the methods for the practice of community management. The use of ORK (Objectives and Key Results) and other methodologies had each 2.1%. Examples of these other methods are Design Thinking and Design Sprint.

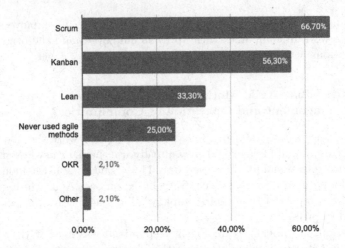

Fig. 4. Main agile methods applied in community management.

Even though we have respondents who claim not to use agile methodologies in managing communities, most companies use project management tools, which were born based on the existing Agile Methods, like Trello[5], Asana[6] and BitBucket[7], for example. In a survey done by Da Silva et al., more than 50% of startups in Pernambuco (Brazil) in the growth phase (called scale ups), use these tools and adopt the agile culture within their teams [12].

Finally, it is possible to observe in Fig. 5 the agile practices most adopted in the day-to-day life of communities of practices and startups. The application of user stories to document and refine what needs to be done appears with 44.4% of responses. The user stories are organized, prioritized and managed using backlogs (77.8%) where the members choose the topics that will be worked on the communities meetings. Retrospectives (66.7%) are also indicated as a very common and often used practice to understand progress of the actions of the groups and how they can improve continuously and systematically their activities. Working in pairs (11.1%) and other practices (33.3%), such as the use of planning poker or review meetings are also part of the results. In this question, respondents could select more than one of the applied practice.

4.3   RQ02: What are the Main Objectives of the Companies and the Aimed Benefits When Adopting Communities?

The massive majority of respondents (91.8%) stated that their organization is involved in some way with communities. This collaboration can be concretized in many different ways. As we can see in Fig. 6, the company itself participates in

---

[5] https://trello.com/pt-BR/about.
[6] https://asana.com/.
[7] https://bitbucket.org/.

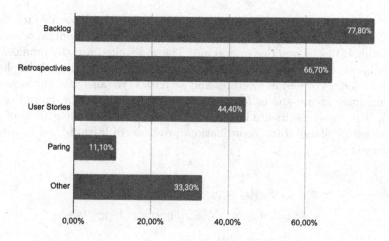

Fig. 5. Main agile practices applied in community management.

business communities (68.8%) or support its employees to collaborate as members of external communities of practice (62.5%). Community support through sponsorship (37.5%) for the promotion of actions or events is also a way to implement the collaboration. Finally, companies have sought to encourage the creation of internal communities of practices to the organization (35.4%). This action is highlighted by the study of Kalenda et al. which relates communities of practice as spaces for learning, knowledge sharing and promotion of best practices for agile teams [9].

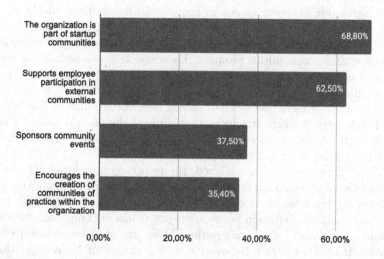

Fig. 6. Ways organizations support communities of practice and startups.

In the cloud of words and expressions shown in Fig. 7 it is possible to observe the main benefits pointed out by respondents in relation to adoption or support from communities of practice or startup. The most cited are the promotion of the collaboration between the members and the potentialization of the sharing of the knowledge covered in meetings and activities. We also have the advantage of communities create spaces for problem solving and focus in innovation. We reaffirm that these results are in line with studies that link the actions of communities with collaboration, coordination, processes of learning and continuous improvement [9].

Safe environment

Adaptability   Recruiting and hiring talent

Innovation   Branding

Problem solving

Partnerships and new businesses

Colaboration

Knowledge sharing

Fig. 7. Benefits for supporting or creating communities of practice and startups.

Another benefit pointed out is that communities promote partnerships and new businesses, through the development of a support network and networking. Thus, it is possible to create spaces for commercial negotiations within the community, positioning of the company with the community, and especially implementing a collaborative culture. A final benefit indicated is the adaptability competence that communities promote. Be connected, promoting the collaboration and engagement with customers, users and other stakeholders is a key point of agile methods, as well as considering changes and part of the product and service development journey [4]. These benefits are also in line with the State of Agile report which concludes that some of the main reasons for adopting agile methods and practices are linked to ability to quickly adapt to changes, reprioritizing what you need be done [5].

In addition to the benefits analyzed, the respondents pointed out the characteristics that better understand defining the purpose of communities within a company or business environment. Figure 8 shows that exchanging experience (87.5%) and collaboration between project teams or companies (68.8%) are important objectives of the communities. These are also considered a place of inspiration (64.6%), where collaboration and exchange of knowledge, through safe learning environments (45.8%), can be enhanced. Finally, communities are spaces for promoting networking and that can also be used for attracting and hiring talents (45.8%) for companies.

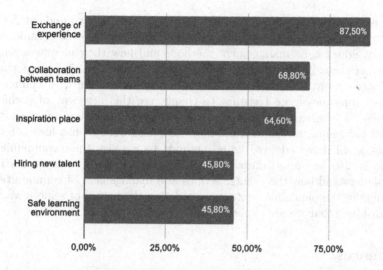

Fig. 8. Objectives of the startup and communities of practice.

5   Conclusion and Future Work

This work aimed to better understand the scenario of community management of startups, practices and business in Brazil and how much the agile methodologies help in managing these collaborative environments.

The study carried out a survey, which had a total of 68 respondents from various states of Brazil, in an investigation conducted to identify the methods and agile practices used in communities and for what purposes they have been used by companies.

The main agile methods used in the communities are Scrum and Kanban, in addition to agile practices such as the use of backlogs, ceremonies of retrospectives and carrying out activities in pair.

Several benefits found in companies that adopt or encourage the creation of communities within their environments. The respondents believe that this can generate better knowledge of scenarios and greater ability to adapt to changes. It is also possible to note that companies that are involved with community actions have a greater engagement with its customers and employees and within the ecosystem of companies, generating a richer networking. Despite this perception we understand that is interesting to develop further investigations on this topic so that we can gather more data and conclusions.

Despite the results presented, it is important to highlight some threats to the validity of this study: (i) the number of respondents could be higher, which would help in a better generalization of the results; (ii) the research focuses on several possible types of communities. It would be interesting to focus on the most used types so that the conclusions could be more specific and useful for the communities; (iii) most of the respondents were from Northeast region (63,2%). It is possible that the answers may have a greater bias in this region of Brazil.

We also think that new studies needs to be carried out to understand more deeply what impact can be generated in communities that, even organic and/or voluntary, adopt agile management methods and how their members replicate these experiences in their work environments. In addition, it is important to know more deeply, how more traditional companies engage with communities and how employees more resistant to change see this new way of exchanging knowledge, sharing experiences and maintaining continuous improvement in professional environments. Understand how companies that do not have a focus or business on IT have adopted agile methods to manage their communities of practice is also an opportunities for future works. Finally, it is interesting to try to understand how the events, actions and management of communities are happening in the pandemic context, considering the period of remote work and social distance that we are experiencing.

References

1. Webber, E.: Building Successful Communities of Practice: Discover How Learning Together Makes Better Organisations. Drew London Limited (2016)
2. Silveira, A., Santino, F., Olivense, H.: Entrepreneurial intention of the participants of the startup weekend: Longitudinal analysis. Int. J. Adv. Manag. Econ. **6**(1), 90–102 (2017)
3. Feld, B..: Startup Communities: Building an Entrepreneurial Ecosystem in Your city. John Wiley & Sons (2020)
4. Fowler, M., Highsmith, J., et al.: The agile manifesto. Softw. Dev. **9**(8), 28–35 (2001)
5. Ai, D.: 14th Annual State of Agile Report (2021) (acessado em 30 de Junho de 2021.https://explore.digital.ai/state-of-agile/14th-annual-state-of-agile-report
6. Palincsar, A.S., Magnusson, S.J., Marano, N., Ford, D., Brown, N.: Designing a community of practice: principles and practices of the GISML community. Teach. Teach. Educ. **14**(1), 5–19 (1998)
7. Bacon, J.: People Powered: How Communities Can Supercharge Your Business, Brand, and Teams. HarperCollins Leadership (2019)
8. Borzillo, S., Schmitt, A., Antino, M.: Communities of practice: keeping the company agile. J. Bus. Strategy **33** (2012)
9. Kalenda, M., Hyna, P., Rossi, B.: Scaling agile in large organizations: practices, challenges, and success factors. J. Softw. Evol. Process **30**(10), e1954 (2018)
10. Molleri, J.S., Petersen, K., Mendes, E.:Survey guidelines in software engineering. In: Proceedings of the 10th ACM/IEEE International Symposium on Empirical Software Engineering and Measurement - ESEM 2016, pp. 1–6 (2016). http://dl.acm.org/citation.cfm?doid=2961111.2962619
11. LinÂker, J., Sulaman, S.M., de Mello, R.M., Hˆst, M., Runeson, P.: Guidelines for conducting surveys in software engineering. Technical report (2015)
12. da Silva, K.T.C., de Farias Junior, I., Moura, H.: Estudo exploratório sobre gerenciamento de projetos em startups pernambucanas. Revista dos Mestrados **8**(2019). ISSN:2317-0115

Scrum in Strongly Hierarchical Organizations: A Literature Review

Fernando Rodrigues de Sá[✉]🆔

Instituto Tecnológico de Aeronáutica (ITA), Praça Marechal do Ar Eduardo Gomes,
No. 50 - Vila das Acácias, São José dos Campos, SP 12228-901, Brazil
desa@ita.br
http://www.ita.br

Abstract. This work aims to present a literature review of the application of Scrum in highly hierarchical organizations. The author initially defined three main bibliographic bases in Computer Science in the search strategy applied to this research, which resulted in 369 articles found. The application of exclusion criteria specified in the study resulted in twelve articles described in this paper. In addition to the twelve articles identified and analyzed through the literature review, this paper also presented other relevant articles about the topic and three previous articles from the author. Despite the apparent contradiction between agile teams with horizontal interaction between their members and organizations based on command and control structures, it is clear that compatibility in the application of agile methods in these strongly hierarchical organizations is possible.

Keywords: Agile methods · Scrum · Hierarchy

1 Introduction

In the 1990s, the popularization of personal computers and the internet increased the demand for software development. Changes in market needs became frequent. Developers were spending more time analyzing how to develop systems than on action. Thus, traditional processes in software development became cumbersome and costly and failed to meet new demands that arose [24].

In February 2001, a group of seventeen people related to software development, unhappy with the software development processes of the time, met at a ski resort in the US state of Utah to seek an alternative to these processes, which no longer met the new demands of the market. The Manifesto for Agile Software Development emerged, composed of four values [3]:

- **Individuals and interactions** over processes and tools;
- **Working software** over comprehensive documentation;
- **Customer collaboration** over contract negotiation; e
- **Responding to change** over following a plan.

C. Rocha et al. (Eds.): WBMA 2021, CCIS 1642, pp. 79–91, 2023.
https://doi.org/10.1007/978-3-031-25648-6_6

The philosophy behind the Manifesto is to value items on the left, highlighted in bold, more than items on the right.

Over time, agile methods have become increasingly popular in software development, and entire organizations have adopted them in managing their activities. In the year 2021, the adoption of agile practices in software development teams increased to 87%, a significant number compared to the 37% registered in the previous year [10].

Despite the increasing popularity of agile methods, organizations still face several challenges in their adoption. Among the most significant barriers to adopting agile practices, the following stand out: Organizational culture in disagreement with agile values; Pervasive resistance to change in organizations; and Insufficient leadership participation [10].

Agile Development Teams are self-managed, so no one tells how team members should do the work. These teams are structured and allowed to organize their work. Also, there is no hierarchy among the [23] team members.

No hierarchy in the horizontal interaction between individuals in agile teams conflicts with conventional structures, such as the one presented by the Classical Management Theory, proposed by Henry Fayol in 1916 [6]. In the company's view, from the administrative management, the unity of command, authority, and responsibility prevails.

This conflict between the horizontal iteration in agile teams and organizations based on command and control results in an apparent incompatibility between agile teams and organizations. So the objective of this research is to present a literature review on works that apply Agile Methods in strongly hierarchical environments.

2   Literature Review

This Section presents works focused on applying agile methods in strongly hierarchical environments. Since these works align with this research's objective, the author defined a search strategy to expand the scope of studies of interest.

2.1   Search Strategy

In the search strategy applied to this research, three of the main bibliographic bases in Computer Science [14] were initially defined to be searched, presented in Table 1.

Table 1. Bibliographic bases used to search for relevant works.

Bibliographic base	Internet address
IEEE Xplore	https://ieeexplore.ieee.org
Scopus	https://scopus.com
Springer Link	https://link.springer.com

Then, the main search terms were defined based on the keywords: **Scrum**; agile; and **hierarch**. Since the keyword agile results in knowledge domains unrelated to this research, the search was performed using the terms **agile development** and **agile methods**. As for the keyword *hierarchy*, due to its origin in the military, the search term *hierarchy* was used with the following variations: **army**; **air force**; **navy**; **military**; and **armed forces**. Thus, the search term used in the search in the bibliographic bases was as follows:

> **(Scrum OR** *agile development* **OR** *agile methods***)**
> **AND**
> **(***hierarchy* **OR army OR** *air force* **OR** *navy* **OR military OR** *armed forces***)**

In the first line of the search term, the group of keywords in parentheses refers to Scrum or other agile methods. In the center line, the logical connective **AND** indicates that the results must contain keywords from both groups, from the first and third lines. The third line presents the group of keywords related to hierarchy and other variations defined in this research. The connective **OR** indicates that in each group, there must be at least one of the keywords of the respective group in the search result. The Table 2 presents the results obtained in each bibliographic database, totaling 369 results found.

Table 2. The number of results from the bibliographic databases searched.

IEEE Xplore	Scopus	Springer Link
48	118	203

The first search in the Springer Link database showed 1022 results, many of which were irrelevant to this literature review. Thus, the search in this database was repeated, considering only results obtained from indexed journals (126) and conferences (77), totaling 203 results, as shown in the table above.

2.2 Exclusion Criteria

The next step was the analysis of titles and abstracts of the total works resulting from the searches carried out to identify the intersection with the theme of this research, in addition to eliminating duplicity of results. The exclusion criteria for articles were:

– Article topic not related to this research (242 excluded results);
– Article addresses other aspects related to agile methods, unrelated to their application in hierarchical environments (87 excluded results);
– Article does not address the application of agile methods, even though it is related to hierarchical environments (4 results excluded);

- Article addresses **acquisition** of software developed by agile methods **for** hierarchical environments (13 results excluded); and
- Article by the same author as this research, which presents results obtained with this research (5 excluded results, referring to 3 different articles).

2.3   Search Results

The exclusion criteria eliminated 351 articles, resulting in the selection of 18 works related to the theme of this research. However, six of them appeared on two different bases. Thus, duplicate articles were disregarded, totaling 12 works in this literature review section. Table 3 presents the total number of articles included in this literature review, those found in duplicate databases, and those excluded.

Table 3. Selection of related works.

Base	Include	Duplicated	Exclude	Total
IEEE Xplore	5	3	40	48
Scopus	5	3	110	118
Springer Link	2	0	201	203
Total	12	6	351	369

The following section presents the syntheses of the works analyzed in this literature review. The first six works presented refer to the adoption of Scrum by the Italian Army.

3   Summary of Works

[7] presented an overview of the adoption of Scrum by the Italian Army for developing software systems using open-source technologies. According to the authors, software systems are very complex in the military environment, and applying agile methods is a challenge.

Scrum defines a high-level approach and mindset for the team that promotes change management and flexibility in work organization to meet customer needs. This work presented the Scrum Team's organization in the Italian Army's specific context.

[7] highlighted that the work in question was just an initial step toward providing a comprehensive analysis of how open-source software and agile methods can be used in this environment, reducing costs and increasing the effectiveness of development teams.

Despite using Scrum for project management, the article's main objective was to present a model to assess the quality level of their development process, seeking affordable solutions based on Free Software.

[18] presented the evolution of the Italian Army's Command and Control (C2) software using agile methods. The introduction of agile in developing highly reliable software was not easy and involved the generation of a new agile methodology called the Italian Army Agile (ITA2).

The introduction of agile in the Italian Army was motivated by faster adaptation to the dynamic needs of missions. A drastic reduction in the defense budget in Italy has also inspired agile adoption.

According to the authors, they dedicated most of the effort to generating an adequate production structure for the system to create an innovative technical and cultural environment. Most of the difficulties encountered in this innovation process were human due to cultural resistance based on consolidated practices.

[19] presented challenges in adopting agile methods in a mixed development team formed by Italian Army soldiers and civilians. Based on agile methodologies, close communication and continuous interaction with the customer allowed the team to become familiar with the complex concepts related to the Intelligence Preparation of the Battlefield (IPB).

Among the challenges, the conflict between team members stood out, considering the rigid military mentality, with disagreements and clashes between members of a hierarchical, organizational, cultural, and sometimes "political" nature.

Despite this, the agile approach allowed the development of valuable listening and empathy skills, which proved to be perfectly aligned with the "democratic" interaction of agile teams. Thus, [19] stated that agile methods led civilians to meet deadlines and scheduled schedules. On the other hand, the military developed a new behavioral attitude that made their relationship with civilians much smoother.

In 4 months, all teams proved capable of cooperating closely and working collaboratively, thus building a virtuous cycle of trust and sharing common goals, which is essential for overcoming challenges. In addition, they created several communication tools to identify user needs, social relationships, and collaborations.

[9] report the need identified by the General Staff of the Italian Army for a strategic management tool for its numerous and extensive infrastructures. The first attempt to find a solution relied on the traditional software engineering approach, which pointed out the difficulty of producing a detailed and accurate requirements document. Implementing a customized software development methodology based on the Agile Scrum Method produced excellent results. The adapted process focused on the relationship between users and developers. As a result, the authors highlighted the reduction of software costs and user satisfaction.

[5] presented a case study of Scrum application in the Italian Army. The project started with one team and, after about one operation, grew to about seven teams, distributed partially and geographically.

The team members were approximately one-third military and two-thirds civilian developers. Most had a master's degree in Computer Science, Computer Engineering, or a related field.

The authors identified resistance to the paradigm shift and the need for support at the highest level to guarantee the continuity of the selected process, despite having positive results.

[5] presents user community governance aspects introduced by [18] created for a structure in which specialists can act as PO, determining the decision-making power of their superiors. This step requires the involvement of high-ranking officials in the Army.

According to [5], the work presented the following originalities:

- The military domain of the study is considerably unexplored in other studies;
- The breadth of experimentation, which took 17 months, starting with 1 team and ending with seven teams; and
- Considering productivity as part of the analysis, with clear evidence of the positive effect of applying agile methods.

[4] summarized the results of the experience of applying agile methods in the defense sector, mainly characterized by embedded and mission-critical software, reported by [5]. The Italian Army approved the project as a pilot to verify the possibility of reducing development costs. At the same time, to produce a product that better responds to changes in the conditions of the theater of operations, where confrontation often becomes asymmetric and requires much faster reaction times than the conventional approach.

After 13 five-week sprints, the team involved in the project delivered a complete product, which met all user requirements, in addition to meeting the regulatory requirements of the Italian Army. A concerted effort was needed to change the development culture to achieve this result. Even counting this effort as part of the development costs, the total costs were lower than those of the traditional development method.

[4] described the results as impressive and reassuring, even with the consequent criticality of the natural resistance to change and the need for support at the highest possible level to ensure the continuity of the process. In summary, the authors identified:

- Increase in productivity with a notable reduction in cost per line of code, compared to the scene before the adoption of agile methods, in addition to a significant increase in tasks developed per Sprint, with a reduction of lines of code per task, as the project advanced;
- Increase in quality, both in terms of defect reduction and in terms of the team's predictive ability, which reached high levels of accuracy; and
- Customer satisfaction, which has reached never before seen levels.

Two articles report the adoption of agile methods in the Israeli Air Force. In the first, [11] presented the facilitation of an XP training for ten Israeli Air Force officers. The team consisted of 60 qualified developers and testers, organized in a hierarchical structure of small groups using short development cycles. The Organization's chain of command supported this work.

Since the team was relatively large and its members had different individual interests, changes in how they carried out the project could not happen overnight but rather in a gradual and carefully planned stage-based process. After the training, they created a specific methodology for implementing XP. As a result of the process, a team started working with XP on a new project, described in the following work.

The second work presented the adoption of XP by the Israeli Air Force to reduce delivery time and increase communication and collaboration with customers in a large and difficult-to-change organization concerning fixed regulations, project approval, management method, and organizational structure [12].

So the project started under close management supervision, with high hopes of being a prototype for implementing XP in other teams on the one hand and fears of XP's incompatibility with the military environment on the other. To deal with this dual perspective, presenting the benefits and pitfalls of the method, an accurate and continuous measurement of the development process was established.

They used two primary research approaches to evaluate the XP implementation process. The first was a qualitative approach to understanding the process from the participants' point of view. The second approach was quantitative, aiming to measure the effectiveness of the process. They collected data through observations, biweekly reflection, and discussion sessions on the process. They also used questionnaires, interviews, and proprietary metrics to communicate which behaviors are most valued or most problematic, enabling faster and more accurate decision-making by project leadership and sharing project information with senior management.

As a result of the qualitative metrics, the more experienced participants emphasized the actual feedback received every two weeks, the fixed delivery dates, the ease of matching inexperienced people to the project, and the way they are aware of problems almost immediately when they occur. Younger participants were satisfied with the communication and direct connection with customers and the process. Most developers wrote the word "people" answering what they liked best.

As for quantitative metrics, managers highlighted the importance of using project progress graphs for decision making and stated that these metrics could help scale XP, for example, to manage multiple teams developing a single large project.

[13] presented the adoption and scale of Scrum in a telecommunications company, guided by standardization and regulated at a national level, with lengthy development cycles. He described the company as a predictable development machine with extensive mechanisms to ensure predictability and control at the expense of flexibility and customer proximity.

The author pointed out that it is necessary to rethink the general approach and address some fundamental, synergistically connected issues to succeed with the organizational architecture. Without addressing all problems, there is a risk of wasted effort. The issues raised were: focus on people, not on technologies or techniques; simplicity; and iterative and incremental work.

The paper presented by [1] suggests enough similarities between the nature of combat in warfare and software development to warrant a comparison between military combat philosophy and the principles of agile software development.

When it comes to war combat, military personnel consider themselves agile. Military command and control are often considered key to rigid, hierarchical decision-making. The phrase "command and control culture" has become common in the agile community to describe rigorous process-centric organizations with centralized authority. However, the military considers tight control to be highly undesirable.

A decentralized command structure bases the military approach on agility, where harmonious initiative achieves unity of purpose. An analysis of military field manuals suggests four synergistic elements underpin the balanced initiative: doctrine, training, leadership, and trust.

For the author, achieving agility depends on the organization's training policies, leadership and development of leaders within the organization, and whether corporate policies encourage or inhibit the emergence of trust. While collaboration, face-to-face conversations, and trust support the Agile Principles, the importance of developing the skills that support these principles is not explicitly stated.

The work presented by [2] reports the experience in contracting Command and Control systems projects acquired by the North Atlantic Treaty Organization (NATO). For managing this type of project, it is necessary to balance the monitoring of traditional metrics of cost, schedule, and scope with risk, value, and quality. In addition, there is the added complexity of obtaining NATO committee approval for all plans and corresponding changes in course. Unlike other hierarchical military environments and democratic alignments, NATO requires complete consensus for decisions, which takes time.

This posed challenges for NATO product managers in acquiring systems using agile processes, which required quick decisions. These challenges become exacerbated when traditional consensus frameworks and change request processes are built around conventional cascading contracts, resulting in conflict.

[17] studied how a medium-sized Finnish company, in the transition to agile methods, managed the development of its software products. Governance roles, responsibilities, and results appeared to be in place at different organizational levels. However, closer inspection revealed challenges in practical implementation. There were many roles and levels of hierarchy with information consistency issues between them. The prioritization of high-level goals was unclear and made it difficult to plan and organize development work based on business value. Tracking from high-level goals to more detailed plans was easily corrupted due to poor planning practices. Monitoring daily work progress was poorly done and not tied to high-level objectives. Consequently, feedback loops were inadequate, making it impossible for management to take timely corrective action.

The authors identified challenges in communication, roles, and responsibilities. The two significant challenges in communication were the lack of communication between PO and their teams and the lack of feedback loops. Roles and responsibilities' challenges embraced the team structure, which conflicted with agile principles; the application of the PO role in a broad and complex context; and the lack of business priorities. Such challenges were mainly related to the governance of the company's software development in the transition to agile methods.

In addition to the twelve articles identified and analyzed through the literature review carried out in this section, the following section presents other relevant works.

4   Complementary Works

[16] made a brief report published on the US Army website about the use of Scrum in one of their organizations, consisting of an adapted model to task and project management process that focuses on transforming products and actions into textitSprints biweekly. The model improved the organization's response time in several ways. As it was an internet article, there were no detailed reports on the model.

[25] recounted how his 10-year experience in the US Navy made him a better SM, highlighting issues surrounding the SM's influence on the team.

[15] presented a comparison between the skills acquired by military veterans that they bring to life, useful in the role of an SM.

A Scrum Master is [15]:

- Facilitator/Communicator;
- Mentor/team coach;
- Impediment remover/troubleshooter;
- Server leader;
- Guardian of the Scrum process; and
- Contact for PO and *Stakeholders*.

A veteran, according to [15]:

- **Has Team Loyalty** - Military personnel carries an intrinsic understanding of how commitment increases team proficiency and builds trust in a work environment. Military personnel generally outperform other candidates in teamwork experience;
- **Has a Credible Work Ethic** - knows the importance of adhering to a process and schedule and consistently performing at work demonstrates professional maturity. Through their services, training, and lifestyle, ex-military personnel typically have a work ethic that sets a standard for teams;
- **Driven by Productivity** - In the workplace, self-discipline is at the heart of self-organizing teams. Soldiers train to work for efficiency, ask for guidance when needed, and exercise self-discipline in professional settings;

- **Has Comprehensive Communication Skills** - Military personnel understand diversity in the workplace and know that good communication needs to be flexible. Most have traveled extensively and understand the nuances of international cultures and communication styles. This awareness, along with technical literacy, can serve to optimize communication efforts across organizations and cultures; and
- **It's an Adaptive Process Follower** - few things are more ingrained in the military than process following. When a process is inadequate, they adapt it as needed and revert to the default process.

In an article posted on the US Air Force Air Education and Training Command website, [20] points out that the term Agile is becoming popular among senior leaders in the Department of Defense. This term was often linked to the importance of developing functional and innovative software that best equips the warrior to respond to uncertain and ever-changing environments.

According to the author, while the private sector adopted Agile long ago, the Department of Defense is starting to incorporate the method into acquisition programs and other projects. In this regard, in the literature review of this Section, I identified six works with reports of software acquisition through agile development for the North American Department of Defense. As it is about the purchase, the works are not about applying agile methods in hierarchical environments of interest to this research.

The following section presents the three previous articles from this author.

5   Previous Articles from this Author

[22] presented the first challenges in adopting agile methods at the Aeronautics Computing Center of São José dos Campos (CCA-SJ). The CCA-SJ is an organization of the Brazilian Air Force (FAB) that develops software systems and flight simulators for the FAB.

In the article, [22] presented the problems encountered in the organization before the adoption of Scrum. To address these problems, the authors applied an Organizational Climate Survey, which pointed out the main factors that contributed to the low level of satisfaction of the CCA-SJ military at the time.

After analyzing the survey results, the authors created and implemented an action plan, which resulted in immediate improvements in the organization's climate.

In the second article, the author presented the lessons learned from adopting Scrum. The main lessons learned presented in the article were [8]:

- Transparency is the key to gaining trust;
- The importance of working top-down and bottom-up approaches simultaneously;
- Reinforcing the importance of applying Scrum values, principles, and practices; and

– A case of success becomes an example for other teams and encourages changes that may occur.

The third article from this author presents the turning point to success in agile adoption: Institutional Support. He also shared teachings from the Brazilian Air Force Pilots to agile teams, and Learning Lessons from the Scrum adoption in the CCA-SJ [21].

6   Final Considerations

This article presented a literature review on applying Scrum in strongly hierarchical organizations. This review showed twelve articles about the topic, in addition to three previous articles from the author.

Despite the apparent contradiction between agile teams with horizontal interaction between their members and organizations based on command and control structures, it is clear that compatibility in the application of agile methods in these strongly hierarchical organizations is possible.

References

1. Adolph, S.: Are we ready to be unleashed? A comparative analysis between agile software development and war fighting. In: Agile Development Conference (ADC 2005), pp. 20–28 (July 2005). https://doi.org/10.1109/ADC.2005.13
2. Aker, S., Audin, C., Lindy, E., Marcelli, L., Massart, J.P., Okur, Y.: Lessons learned and challenges of developing the NATO air command and control information services. In: 2013 IEEE International Systems Conference (SysCon), pp. 791–800 (April 2013). https://doi.org/10.1109/SysCon.2013.6549974
3. Beck, K., et al.: Manifesto for Agile Software Development Twelve Principles of Agile Software (2001). http://www.agilemanifesto.org
4. Benedicenti, L., Messina, A., Sillitti, A.: Iagile: mission critical military software development. In: Proceedings - 2017 International Conference on High Performance Computing and Simulation, HPCS 2017, pp. 545–552 (2017). https://doi.org/10.1109/HPCS.2017.87
5. Benedicenti, L., et al.: Applying scrum to the army: a case study. In: Proceedings - International Conference on Software Engineering, pp. 725–727 (2016). https://doi.org/10.1145/2889160.2892652
6. Chiavenato, I.: Introdução à Teoria Geral da Administração, 2nd edn. Campus, Rio de Janeiro (2000)
7. Cotugno, F.R., Messina, A.: Adapting SCRUM to the Italian army: methods and (open) tools. IFIP Adv. Inf. Commun. Technol. **427**, 61–69 (2014). https://doi.org/10.1007/978-3-642-55128-4_7
8. de Sá, F.R., Vieira, R.G., da Cunha, A.M.: Lessons learned from the agile transformation of an aeronautics computing center. In: Meirelles, P., Nelson, M.A., Rocha, C. (eds.) WBMA 2019. CCIS, vol. 1106, pp. 85–91. Springer, Cham (2019). https://doi.org/10.1007/978-3-030-36701-5_7

9. Dettori, D., Salomoni, S., Sanzari, V., Trenta, D., Ventrelli, C.: Ita army agile software implementation of the LC2EVO army infrastructure strategic management tool. In: Ciancarini, P., Sillitti, A., Succi, G., Messina, A. (eds.) Proceedings of 4th International Conference in Software Engineering for Defence Applications. AISC, vol. 422, pp. 35–50. Springer, Cham (2016). https://doi.org/10.1007/978-3-319-27896-4_4

10. Digital.ai: 15th Annual State Of Agile Report | Digital.ai. Tech. rep., Digital.ai (2021). https://digital.ai/resource-center/analyst-reports/state-of-agile-report

11. Dubinsky, Y., Hazzan, O., Keren, A.: Introducing extreme programming into a software project at the Israeli air force. In: Baumeister, H., Marchesi, M., Holcombe, M. (eds.) XP 2005. LNCS, vol. 3556, pp. 19–27. Springer, Heidelberg (2005). https://doi.org/10.1007/11499053_3

12. Dubinsky, Y., Talby, D., Hazzan, O., Keren, A.: Agile metrics at the Israeli Air Force. In: Agile Development Conference (ADC 2005), pp. 12–19 (2005). https://doi.org/10.1109/ADC.2005.8

13. Duka, D.: Adoption of agile methodology in software development. In: 2013 36th International Convention on Information and Communication Technology, Electronics and Microelectronics (MIPRO), pp. 426–430 (May 2013)

14. Felizardo, K., Nakagawa, E., Fabbri, S., Ferrari, F.: Revisao sistematica da literatura em engenharia de software: teoria e pratica, 1st edn. Elsevier, Rio de Janeiro (2017)

15. Friend, T.: Why Military Veterans Make Great Scrum Masters (2014). http://blog.eliassen.com/why-military-veterans-make-great-scrum-masters

16. Horton, J.: Scrum is the word in the 193rd (2015). https://www.army.mil/article/145252/scrum_is_the_word_in_the_193rd

17. Lehto, I., Rautiainen, K.: Software development governance challenges of a middle-sized company in agile transition. In: 2009 ICSE Workshop on Software Development Governance, pp. 36–39 (May 2009). https://doi.org/10.1109/SDG.2009.5071335

18. Messina, A., Fiore, F.: The Italian Army C2 evolution: from the current SIAC-CON2 land command & control system to the LC2EVO using agile software development methodology. In: 2016 International Conference on Military Communications and Information Systems, ICMCIS 2016, pp. 1–8 (2016). https://doi.org/10.1109/ICMCIS.2016.7496585

19. Gazzerro, S., Muschitiello, A.F., Pasqui, C.: Agile Plus New army diffused and shared leadership. In: Ciancarini, P., Sillitti, A., Succi, G., Messina, A. (eds.) Proceedings of 4th International Conference in Software Engineering for Defence Applications. AISC, vol. 422, pp. 163–179. Springer, Cham (2016). https://doi.org/10.1007/978-3-319-27896-4_14

20. Poland, C.: The Air Force is becoming more Agile - one project at a time (2019). https://www.aetc.af.mil/News/Article/1823544/the-air-force-is-becoming-more-agile-one-project-at-a-time/

21. de Sa, F.R., Godoi Vieira, R., Cunha, A.M.d.: Learning lessons from the scrum adoption in the Brazilian Air Force. IT Profes. 24(1), 49–55 (2022). https://doi.org/10.1109/MITP.2021.3132310, https://ieeexplore.ieee.org/document/9717273/

22. de Sá, F.R., de Resende Lucas, E.L., de Oliveira, A.D.: Scrum in a strongly hierarchical organization. In: Tonin, G.S., Estácio, B., Goldman, A., Guerra, E. (eds.) WBMA 2018. CCIS, vol. 981, pp. 97–102. Springer, Cham (2019). https://doi.org/10.1007/978-3-030-14310-7_7

23. Schwaber, K., Sutherland, J.: The Scrum Guide The Definitive Guide to Scrum: The Rules of the Game. Tech. rep., Scrum.org (2020)

24. Sommerville, I.: Engenharia de Software, 9th edn. Pearson Prentice Hall, São Paulo (2011)
25. Wortham, T.: How Military Tactics Made Me a Better Scrum Master (2014). https://www.spikesandstories.com/how-military-tactics-made-me-a-better-scrum-master/

Short Papers

Experience in Implementing the Scrum Framework in Incubated Companies

Ludimila Monjardim Casagrande(✉)

Apoema Consulting and Training, Vitória, ES, Brazil
ludimila.casagrande@apoemaconsultoria.com.br

Abstract. This article presents the experience of implementing the Scrum framework in incubated companies in the Information Technology field. The main goal of this study was to demystify the idea that a senior team is required for the application and good performance of Scrum. Another goal was to verify the time needed for companies to start using the framework and to identify the time it takes for teams to achieve stability in the project. In addition, we observed the velocity rates, if there was an increase in velocity during the project execution, and we also inspected the differences between what was planned and what was performed. In terms of methodology, this is a case study performed by market professionals.

Keywords: Scrum · Project management · Agile development · Velocity rates

1 Introduction

There are some frequent concerns and issues related to Scrum, especially for those who are getting introduced to this framework for the first time. When they are presented to the Scrum framework, many directors and managers think that a senior team is needed to make self-organization – one of the framework's key practices. They believe that only very experienced professionals are capable of managing their own work and having the autonomy to make decisions without having to consult with an immediate supervisor. Many practical experiences, however, show that this impression is actually a myth, and this is a fact that is demonstrated in this report.

Many people also do not believe in the promised increase in the development velocity, given the fact that the proposed Scrum framework includes four formal ceremonies or events. Since they are familiar with endless and unproductive meetings, it is natural for them to feel that way. However, all Scrum elements have a clear purpose, with a limited duration, and are strongly based on research, data, and experience as described in [1].

Other common concerns are related to the time needed to train the team and to implement Scrum, in addition to the time needed to achieve stability in the project given the new way of managing and working.

Therefore, this article reports the experience of implementing Scrum in incubated companies and presents information regarding the aforementioned issues.

© Springer Nature Switzerland AG 2023
C. Rocha et al. (Eds.): WBMA 2021, CCIS 1642, pp. 95–102, 2023.
https://doi.org/10.1007/978-3-031-25648-6_7

2   Context

In 2017/2018, the Apoema Consulting and Training company developed a training and support project for Scrum implementation in three technology-based companies incubated at TecVitória – the largest business incubator in the state of Espírito Santo, Brazil.

In addition to providing companies with management innovation, one of the project's goals was to observe people's behavior and the result of applying Scrum in companies still in formation and with inexperienced teams.

Two cases with quite different characteristics were selected and are reported in this article. The names of companies will be omitted to safeguard them and to present the cases in greater detail.

In Case 1, the company was a software factory, and the customer was off-site and a large-scale business. The project was also large-scale, considering the scope size, and critical to the end customer. The supplier (incubated) company had practically no experience with Scrum, but already knew a little about it. The project was developed by a predominantly junior team, mostly composed of 4 developers, including 3 interns, and growing to 6 developers (4 interns) at particular times. The company's track record included projects that had exceeded their initial budget by 50–100%; therefore, the company was looking for a solution to keep the project costs within the planned contingency or, at the very least, to reduce losses. The projects were carried out according to the traditional management approach. This company shall be named Company 1 henceforth.

The context of Case 2 is quite different from the first. In this case, the software product belonged to the company itself and therefore the customer or main provider of requirements was in-house. The system was already in production and had several off-site customers, who eventually requested changes and bug fixes. Corrective changes needed to be prioritized because the system was already in production, which usually negatively affected the planning of team activities.

The CEO, the CTO, and the lead of the support team were looking for a management solution with the main goal of organizing the development activities so that it was possible to make the required corrections, meet the demands of the customers and the internal demands for efficient system improvements. A second goal was to increase team velocity.

3   Theoretical Background

Scrum is a lightweight framework that helps people, teams, and businesses generate value through adaptive solutions for complex problems [2]. Thus, Scrum suggests a structure to organize the work and to increase the performance of agile teams so that they can make frequent deliveries, in the shortest possible time and in order to efficiently respond to constant change requests.

Scrum follows an iterative and incremental development approach to enable quick and frequent product increment deliveries, and to improve the predictability and risk control, since the customer feedback is collected constantly and at short intervals, and there is an evolution of the product at each iteration which, in Scrum, is called Sprint [3].

There are three roles in Scrum, each with different responsibilities within the Scrum Team, namely: Developers, Product Owner, and Scrum Master.

In summary, Scrum requires a Scrum Master to promote an environment where: (1) a Product Owner orders the work for a complex problem into a Product Backlog (list of product features or to-do items); (2) the Scrum Team turns a selection of the work into an Increment of Value during a Sprint and (3) the Scrum Team and its stakeholders inspect the results and adjust for the next Sprint [2].

Relevant information that can assist teams in implementing Scrum can be found at [4] and [5].

4 Methodology

To start the agile project management in a company, the Scrum authors Ken Schwaber and Jeff Sutherland recommend the selection of a pilot project, and the application of the Scrum framework only to this particular project at the first moment [4]. Following this recommendation is important because adopting any agile management approach, in general, requires a cultural change, which is also called a mindset change, especially in cases where the company is used to following a traditional management approach such as practices recommended by PMI/PMBOK, for example.

Due to this adaptation need, it is important to promote changes gradually. In addition, it is common to have some resistance from team members, from the client, and even from managers in some cases.

In Company 1, the vast majority of projects were developed for the same customer; and, following the recommendation of the Scrum authors, one of these projects was chosen as a pilot. The criterion that determined this choice was the existence of a poorly detailed scope, subject to many changes, and a high degree of uncertainty regarding the requirements and operation of some of the system modules; in addition, the recurring incidence of not meeting deadlines and cost overruns in projects developed specifically for that customer. When the consultancy was hired, the project had already been marketed in the traditional management terms, that is, with a closed deal regarding scope, deadline, and cost. The supplier company, however, opted for an agile execution in order to minimize risks and possible losses.

Company 2 only had one system, and, in this case, there was no need to choose.

In both cases, all members of the development teams of the selected projects and their superiors (considering the companies' functional hierarchies) attended a 20-h training about the agility concept and the Scrum framework. By doing that, an alignment of all involved people was obtained regarding the new management proposal and the new way of organizing the projects' work.

During the training, the most controversial points, such as open scope, flexibility regarding changes, the team's self-organization, the non-existence of a project manager were pointed out and widely discussed.

The second step was to sensitize the external client (in Case 1) about the benefits that could be achieved by adopting Scrum and the alignment regarding their role and responsibilities in the project. The presentation of the benefits was based on research data found in [6, 7], and [8]. The involvement of the hierarchical superiors in the training stage and the sensitizing of the external client were based on the fact that the aspects of "executive management support" and "user (customer) involvement" were identified as critical factors for the success of IT projects in the research accomplished by the Standish Group [6].

The third step, in both cases, was a brief project setup stage, where preliminary decisions were made and when there was a discussion about the stages of the process development or workflow, the standard sprint duration, the definition of done, the columns that should compose the Kanban board, the management tools to be adopted, the measurement units to be used for activities and tasks, the ideal team size, the required skills, and competences, among other relevant aspects to start the project. At this point, the teams also defined who would be the Scrum Master and Product Owner of each project, and the acquisition and configuration of the adopted tools were carried out.

The fourth step was the actual start of Scrum execution. In both cases, all events were monitored during the initial sprints by Apoema's consultant, who offered support and cleared up questions about the correct application of the framework, and all events were carried out in accordance with what is recommended in the official Scrum guide [2, 3], and based on the agile development principles [9, 10].

5 Presentation and Analysis of Results

5.1 Case 1

As previously mentioned, the project in Case 1 was marketed following the traditional approach, that is, with closed scope, cost, and deadline, and was selected by the supplier company as a pilot project for agile execution using Scrum, aiming to reduce losses with delays and reworking.

The time between the end of the team training and the beginning of the first sprint, that is, the time it took to properly start the execution of Scrum was one month because the project was planned in the traditional way and due to the need to sensitize the external client, which was quite conservative.

The sprints lasted for 15 days, and the project development team was predominantly junior, mostly composed of 4 developers, up to 6 developers at certain times. The team's previous experience in Scrum projects was next to null. The entire team completed Apoema's 20-h training before starting the project, including the company's CEO and CTO.

What could be observed by analyzing the velocity graphs (Fig. 1, Fig. 2), extracted from the Jira management tool, is a low rate of team velocity during the first 3 sprints, that is, during the first 45 days of the project, which was expected due to the team's adaptation to the new management model, new technologies that were adopted in the project and the practice of implementing automated tests, which had never been done in the company before.

By better adjusting the planning to the actual capacity shown by the team, the predicted goal was reached in Sprint 4 (Table 1). From this point on, the team started to perform well above the initial sprints and achieved the goal again in Sprint 6 (Table 2). It can also be observed that the team starts from a rate of 22 points in the first sprint and

Table 1. Results achieved in sprints 1 to 5 of Case 1.

	Sprint 1	Sprint 2	Sprint 3	Sprint 4	Sprint 5
Total planned points	47	42	48	36	53
Total completed points	22	29	21	36	50
Average rate in points	22	25.5	24.0	27.0	31.6

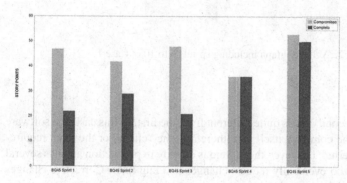

Fig. 1. Velocity graph including sprints 1 to 5 of Case 1.

Table 2. Results achieved in sprints 6 to 10 of Case 1.

	Sprint 6	Sprint 7	Sprint 8	Sprint 9	Sprint 10
Total planned points	57	42	49	51	50
Total completed points	57	35	38	52	44
Average rate in points	35.8	35.7	36.0	37.8	38.4

reaches a total average rate of 38.4 points in Sprint 10. In addition, the velocity rate is 31.6 points in sprints 1 to 5 and becomes 45.2 points in sprints 6 to 10, which proves the increase in velocity in just 5 months of Scrum implementation and use.

Another fundamental aspect that needs to be analyzed is the difference between what was planned and what was carried out, as this factor determines the rate of delay and extra costs of the project. In this case, the average rate of unreached points was 19.5%, considering the 10 sprints, and it was only 10% if we consider the last 5 analyzed sprints. Assuming that the project's contingency rate is 20%, which is a commonly practiced value, the actual rate presented is within predicted, even given the team's inexperience with the agile approach, with the automated tests, and some of the adopted technologies.

The most significant fluctuations in the planned values occurred due to holidays or the eventual allocation of more developers to the project in certain sprints.

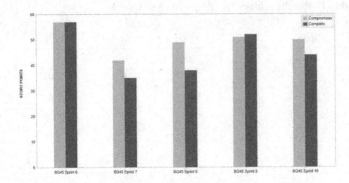

Fig. 2. Velocity graph including sprints 6 to 10 of Case 1.

5.2 Case 2

The context of this second case is quite different from the first. In this case, the software product belongs to the company itself and, therefore, the "client" or the main requirements provider is internal. However, the system is already in production and has several off-site customers, who eventually request changes and bug fixes. Corrective changes need to be prioritized because the system is already in use, which often affects the planning of team activities.

The company's CEO and CTO, the person responsible for the support team and the development team chose to adopt the Scrum framework with the main goal of organizing the development activities so that it was possible to make the necessary corrections, meet customer demands and internal demands for system improvements. A second goal was to increase team velocity.

Before starting the implementation, all development team members, the CTO, the CEO, and the support team lead completed Apoema's 20-h training. The implementation started one week after the end of the training.

A sprint length of 15 days was chosen, and the team consisted of 1 senior developer and 2 interns. The team's previous experience with Scrum projects was limited.

After a troubled start that lasted about 2 months (4 sprints), with sudden fluctuations in performance caused mainly by the high cumulative number of bugs to be fixed and changes in the scope of the sprints, the team's work finally began to reach the desired stability from Sprint 5 onwards, when the planned goal was exceeded, as can be seen in the velocity graph (Fig. 3). From there, the team finds its balance point and maintains an average velocity rate of 33.6 points completed per cycle (Table 3) in the final 7 sprints analyzed (5 to 11); in the first 5 sprints, the average was 22.5 points (value reported by the team). This demonstrates, once again, the velocity gain and the achieved level of organization with the adoption of Scrum.

By analyzing the difference between what was planned and the actual results, which are related to the excess cost of product development, it appears that the average rate of unrealized points was 6%, if we consider sprints from 5 to 11, and 17%, if we consider the last 5 sprints (7 to 11), which are below the usual 20% contingency rate.

Table 3. Results achieved in sprints 5 to 11 of Case 2.

	Sprint 5	Sprint 6	Sprint 7	Sprint 8	Sprint 9	Sprint 10	Sprint 11
Total planned points	19	35	37	40	45	42	44
Total completed points	26	38	36	35	32	36	32
Average rate in points	26	32	33.3	33.8	33.4	33.8	33.6

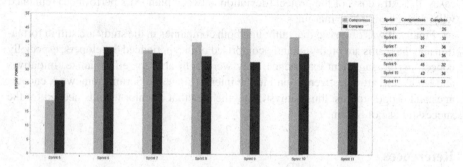

Fig. 3. Velocity graph including sprints 5 to 11 of Case 2.

It is also observed in this case that there is an attempt to increase the team's velocity by increasing the planned work, especially from Sprint 8. What is found, however, after successive sprints, is that the team is not able to achieve a result higher than 38 points, which is, therefore, the limit of its capacity. In this case, the ideal is to adjust the planning to the identified capacity of this team. If there is a real need to complete a higher number of points per sprint, the results indicate that it is necessary to allocate one more developer to achieve the goals.

In all cases, the correct use of Scrum (considering the framework rules described in the official guide) and a good management tool, such as Jira, for example, provide valuable information to track the project progress and deviations for proper decision-making.

6   Conclusion

Therefore, as an answer to the investigation questions, the time needed to set up the project and to start the Scrum execution, after training the team, was one month in Case 1 and only one week in Case 2. In all implementation cases supported by Apoema Consulting, it was never necessary a setup time superior to one month (this information is based on our experience in implementing the Scrum framework over the last 5 years).

As for the time to reach stability, in Case 1 this occurred after 45 days after the start of the Scrum execution, and in Case 2, after 2 months. In the overall experience at Apoema Consulting, the maximum time to reach stability was 3 months. This time period depends on the nature and complexity of the project, both in terms of requirements and regarding the technologies used, in addition, of course, to the experience and level of knowledge of the team members.

In both cases, the team's velocity gains were observed during the course of the project. In Case 1, the team started from an average rate of 24 completed points per sprint in the first 3 sprints and reached an average rate of 38.4 points per sprint in the first 10 sprints of the project. In Case 2, the team starts from an average rate of 22.5 points completed per sprint in the first 5 sprints and reaches an average velocity of 33.6 points completed per iteration in the last 7 analyzed sprints (5 to 11). Furthermore, in both cases, the extra costs of the project (deviation between planned x performed) remained within the contingency margin.

Finally, it was observed that, although both companies in the study are still in formation and the teams are predominantly comprised of inexperienced developers, especially concerning management experience, they were both able to self-organize. Initiatives and leadership attitudes were found in the interns, since the Scrum framework encourages and is open to this, thus demystifying the idea that a senior team is needed for the successful use of Scrum.

References

1. Sutherland, J.; Sutherland, J.J.: Scrum: the Art of Doing Twice the Work in Half the Time. Currency. Penguin Random House, New York City (2014)
2. Schwaber, K., Sutherland, J.: The Scrum Guide - The Definitive Guide to Scrum: the Rules of the Game. Scrum.org. (2020)
3. Schwaber, K., Sutherland, J.: The Scrum Guide - The Definitive Guide to Scrum: The Rules of the Game (2017)
4. Schwaber, K., Sutherland, J.: Software in 30 Days: How Agile Managers Beat the Odds, Delight Their Customers, and Leave Competitors in the Dust. Wiley, New Jersey (2012)
5. Sabbagh, R.: Scrum: gestão ágil para projetos de sucesso. Casa do Código, São Paulo (2013)
6. Project Smart: The Standish Group Chaos Report 2014. https://www.projectsmart.co.uk/white-papers/chaos-report.pdf. Accessed 12 June 2021
7. Scrum Alliance: The 2016 State of Scrum Report (2016)
8. VersionOne: 11th Annual State of Agile™ Report, 2017. https://stateofagile.com/#ufh-c-702 7494-state-of-agile. Accessed 12 June 2021
9. Beck, K., Schwaber, K., Sutherland, J. et al.: Principles Behind the Agile Manifesto (2001). http://agilemanifesto.org/principles.html. Accessed 12 June 2021
10. Scrum.org. The Home of Scrum: What is Scrum? https://www.scrum.org/resources/what-is-scrum. Accessed 12 June 2021

Study of a Software Development Team's Adaptations to Remote Work During the COVID-19 Pandemic

Diego A. S. Lisbôa[✉], Thayssa A. da Rocha[✉], Letícia S. Machado[✉],
Clara M. Caldeira[✉], and Cleidson R. B. de Souza[✉]

Federal University of Pará, Belém, Brazil
diegolisboa@ufpa.br, thayssa.tocha@icen.ufpa.br,
leticia.smachado@gmail.com, cmarque@iu.edu,
cleidson.desouza@acm.org

Abstract. The social distancing practices adopted to contain the spread of the COVID-19 pandemic led many companies to migrate to remote work in a compulsory and unplanned way. This sudden transition to working from home has caused profound changes in personal and professional relationships. In this paper, we present the results of a qualitative observational study about the adaptations made in the software process activities of a software development coordinator of a Brazilian university. These adaptations aimed to support the transition to remote work during the pandemic, without letting the organization lose its essence in adopting agile practices. These adaptations were analyzed based on the technical aspects (hard skills) and behavioral aspects (soft skills) of the employees of the researched organization.

Keywords: Adaptation · Agile practices · Remote work · Pandemic

1 Introduction

Software development has long been recognized by researchers [1] as a social activity. Practitioners also recognize the importance of interaction between those involved in software development activities, as explained in the first value of the agile manifesto: "individuals and interactions more than processes and tools". The third agile value also points to the importance of collaboration between members: "collaboration with the customer more than contract negotiation" [2].

In 2020, the whole world was surprised by the coronavirus pandemic (COVID-19), which brought with it various restrictions on interactions between people, causing profound changes in the personal and professional lives of individuals. In this context, many companies have been forced to work remotely in a very short period of time. In this scenario, people are working remotely, but not in an office or prepared environment, but from their beds, kitchen tables, sofas and with all their families promoting interruptions, needing assistance, etc. [3].

C. Rocha et al. (Eds.): WBMA 2021, CCIS 1642, pp. 103–109, 2023.
https://doi.org/10.1007/978-3-031-25648-6_8

This paper describes a work in progress on the adaptations made to the software process activities of a Brazilian university coordination called COTIC and its transition to remote working during the COVID-19. The technical and behavioral aspects of COTIC employees were used in this research as an analytical lens to "evaluate" how effective adaptations were in supporting the remote work process during the pandemic and in helping to maintain the adoption of agile practices.

2   Context and Methodology

The name of the researched organization is COTIC. Its objective is the development of software systems required by one of the university's departments. It also provides support to the systems in its existing portfolio of projects. During the research phase, the team was composed of ten people, organized according to and using the practices of the Scrum framework [4].

The methodology used was qualitative empirical research, by means of participative observation of the work process of the COTIC team. This was possible because one of the authors is a COTIC employee and is part of the team. The data collection phase took place from March to December 2020, and all its main activities were carried out remotely during this period.

Data collection was conducted through participant observation of the team's work routine, including interactions between the team and its stakeholders. Field notes were prepared based on records of conversations from communication tools; activities documented in collective project management tools; artifacts stored in the shared repository; and feedback from participants in retrospective and other meetings.

Hard skills are the technical requirements and knowledge that a person must have to perform a task. These include the theoretical foundations and practical exposure that an individual must have to successfully perform the planned task. Soft skills, on the other hand, have their roots in psychology and cover a wide range of characteristics involving personality types, social interaction skills, communication, and personal habits [5].

3   COTIC's Software Process Before the Pandemic

COTIC's software development process consists of seven activities, as shown below:

3.1   Build Comprehensive Model

This activity aims to align with the stakeholders the ideas regarding the minimum viable product to be built and its increments. The participants in this activity, used tools such as whiteboard, flip-charts and post-it's.

3.2   Plan Releases

This activity aims to define the sequence in which the product's functionalities will be delivered. The participants of this activity used as main tool the physical framework called MVP Canvas.

3.3 Build Product Backlog

This activity aims to create and elaborate an effective and collaborative product backlog. The participants of this activity used as main tool the physical framework called PBB Canvas.

3.4 Run Sprint

This activity is related to the execution of the Sprints for building the product. The participants of this activity used tools such as: User Stories cards on post-it notes; Kanban board for visual management of the work progress; Adobe XD and Bizagi tools for prototyping and modeling; Eclipse IDE and PhpMyAd-min for software development and database management; GitLab for version control; and Cypress for automated testing.

3.5 Upgrade Product Version

This activity aims to integrate the code of the User Stories developed to make the version available for approval. The participants of this activity use the GIT-FTP tool as the main tool.

3.6 Homologate Product Version

This activity aims to present a new version of the software product to the Product Owner, in a homologation environment, for evaluation. The participants of this activity used User Stories cards as the main tool.

3.7 Deliver Product Version

This activity aims to make the new version of the product available to end users in a production environment. The participants of this activity used GIT-FTP as their main tool.

3.8 Considerations

The high-level description of the COTIC software development process presented in this chapter allows for some observations. First, it is possible to identify the performance of various coordination and alignment activities in person with the entire team. In addition, we can see the use of tools that require the presence of everyone in the same shared physical space. For example, release planning requires the collaborative construction of an artifact (Canvas MVP), using a physical board and post-it's. Other examples of similar activities and their respective artifacts include: (i) the construction of the Product Backlog, generating the PBB Canvas as an artifact; (ii) the Sprint planning meeting, generating the Sprint Backlog as an artifact; (iii) the daily meetings between the Scrum Team members, generating the planning of the day's activities as an artifact; (iv) and the Sprint retrospective meetings, generating as an artifact a kanban board containing the main information discussed in the meeting. With the COVID-19 pandemic and the need for social isolation, this process has been modified as will be described in the next chapter.

4   COTIC's Software Process During the Pandemic

With the sudden migration to remote working, adaptations were necessary for the execution of the existing software development process. As a COTIC employee, the first author of this paper was responsible for adapting this process while maintaining agile software development practices but adapted for the remote work context. In general, it was observed that the process activities and those responsible for their execution remained unchanged.

During the stages of the Build Comprehensive Model, Plan Releases, Build Product Backlog and Approve Product Version process, the meetings between the people responsible for the tasks were held by videoconference through the Google Meet tool. The Google Drive tool was adopted for file sharing during the entire remote work process.

In the Build Comprehensive Model and Plan Releases activities, with the limitation of using physical boards, the Web Mural tool with the Lean Inception theme [6] was adopted for visual management of these activities, allowing simultaneous collaboration of members to the virtual board.

To build the Product Backlog, the Web Mural tool was again used with the Product backlog Canvas template [7], to visually manage the activities. In addition, the Trello tool was used to organize the Product Backlog items generated in this activity. This tool was also used during the execution of the Sprint. For the internal communication among the members of the agile team, the Discord tool was used, which allows the use of voice over IP and the creation of communication channels via text, audio, and videoconferences. At COTIC the channels are organized by project, plus the socialization and technical and business support channels offering access and free contribution at any time of the day to all internal COTIC members (Scrum Master, Product Owner, Scrum Team). The socialization channel, called #topic-off, was used for informal conversations among the members of the agile team, with links to courses and training, information about the COVID-19 pan-demy and general topics. The technical support and business channels, called #help-technical and #help- business, were used for technical questions and to understand the business rules of the User Stories, respectively. All channels were used by the team, being the #topic-off the most frequent, especially for updating information about the pandemic, including the vaccine.

The activities related to the construction of the User Stories were performed in pairs, assigned in the Trello tool according to the availability information in the pairing spreadsheet available on Google Drive. On the other hand, the retrospective meetings were held with the help of the FunRetro tool that allows the visual management of the Sprint retrospective ceremony, registration of the participants' information and organization of the meeting duration. We also started to use other GitLab resources, such as Wiki, for knowledge management: Scrum Team members recorded the standard procedures for the execution of certain activities, allowing collaborators to have access to this content, in case required.

In the activities of Increment and Deliver Product Version, communication between the team was carried out via Discord and the Trello tool was used to indicate the User Stories that were part of the product version. Relevant artifacts were shared via Google Drive so that everyone involved could access and contribute. Finally, in the Product

Version Approval activity, the Trello tool was used to manage User Stories and any changes, defects and improvements requested by the Product Owner.

5   Results

The results observed in this research will be presented according to the technical and behavioral abilities of COTIC's employees.

5.1   Hard Skills

- Use of collaborative tools that enable quick feedbacks and visual management of information, such as: Wall Tool for the dynamics of conception and elaboration of the product Backlog; Trello used as the team's task board; Discord for communication among team members; and FunRetro for the team's retrospective dynamics.
- Flexibility in the workload of the Scrum Team members, based on the pairing's spreadsheet, allowing greater coupling for development tasks, such as pair programming and programming Dojos; It was also observed the use of knowledge management tools to register tasks that for some reason, are not performed in pairs. In this way, if it is necessary to perform the task again, any member of the team can try to solve it.
- Creation, in the Discord tool, of specific channels for collaboration among the team, in addition to the use of the pairing spreadsheet, covering all members of the Scrum Team, which helped to foster an environment conducive to cooperation and collaboration.
- It was also observed that in the team's retrospective meetings, questions were included regarding the good use of the collaborative tools and if there were any difficulties in using them.
- Support from top management for this adaptation of the process, the use of collaborative tools to be used, besides its self-organization for managing the workload of its collaborators and for adapting its work process by keeping the adoption of agile software development practices; Another aspect observed was the creation of a practice guide for the transition to remote work. This guide should contain organizational guidelines and tips for the proper use of collaborative tools and the steps of the work process tasks.

5.2   Soft Skills

- Increased number of remote meetings with shorter duration time (two hours maximum) for inspection and alignment of activities; Also observed was an increase in the daily frequency of feedbacks, help and support among employees; Another relevant factor was the importance of meetings being held preferably with the cameras on, because gestures and facial expressions also contribute to a good common understanding between members.
- Decrease in the learning curve among less experienced members, making it easier for new members to adapt to the activities; The flexibility of the workload also provided a greater sense of trust in the team, because team members who in the face-to-face model worked different shifts, could have the chance to work together on development tasks,

sharing technical learning and life experiences; It was also observed the importance of the pairings spreadsheet organization, to avoid the creation of subgroups within the team. This organization is also important so that the allocation of tasks is done proportionally to the level of knowledge of the pairs.

- Socialization channels, created in the Discord tool, allowed informal and spontaneous communication among team members to exchange knowledge, feedbacks and to try to minimize, as far as possible, the stress and the feeling of isolation caused by the pandemic. In this sense, employees were oriented about the balance between professional and personal life to maintain a sustainable remote work routine.
- Large number of interruptions due to physical and logical infrastructure problems; There were also reported situations of members with health problems, such as back pain and eye problems, which were most likely caused by the poor ergonomics of the employees' homework environment.
- Another important characteristic is to have more sensitivity and common sense for the pressure to deliver demands and to charge for higher productivity in this pandemic period, because we are not in a context of common remote work, but in a pandemic context, where each employee can deal with the situation in different ways. These pressures, if not well managed, can cause an environment of tension and attrition among team members.

6 Conclusion

The main contribution of this work was to present adaptations made to the work process of an information technology team in a department of a Brazilian university. These adaptations were necessary due to the sudden and mandatory transition to remote work needed to help maintain social distance during the COVID-19 pandemic. We also presented some of the adaptations observed in relation to agile software development practices, both from the technical (hard skills) and behavioral (soft skills) points of view of its collaborators.

As future work, it would be interesting to consider how effective these adaptations in the software process were from the point of view of productivity in the context of the observed team, as well as the team's perception regarding satisfaction with these adaptations.

References

1. Curtis, B., Krasner, H., et al.: A field study of the software design process for large systems. Commun. ACM **31**(11), 1268–1287 (1988)
2. Agile Manifesto. http://agilemanifesto.org/. Accessed 10 May 2021
3. Ralph, P., Baltes, S., Adisaputri, G., et al.: Pandemic programming. Empir. Softw. Eng. **25**(6), 4927–4961 (2020)
4. Schwaber, K., Sutherland, J.: The Scrum Guide. <https://www.scrum-guides.org/docs/scrumg uide/v2020/2020-Scrum-Guide-PortugueseBR-2.0.0.pdf>. Accessed 26 May 2021
5. Ahmed, F., Capretz, L.F., Bouktif, S., Campbell, P.: Soft skills and software development: a reflection from software industry. Int. J. Inf. Processing Manag. **4**, 171–191 (2013)

6. Caroli, P.: Lean Inception: Como alinhar pessoas e construir o produto certo. Edição 1. São Paulo, Editora Caroli (2018)
7. Aguiar, F., Caroli, P.: Product Backlog Building: Um guia prático para criação e refinamento de backlog para produtos de sucesso. Edição 1. São Paulo, Editora Caroli (2021)

Agile Requirements Engineering Practices: A Survey in Brazilian Software Development Companies

Juan Carlos Barata[1]([⊠]), Diego Lisboa[2]([⊠]), Laudelino Cordeiro Bastos[1]([⊠]),
and Adolfo Neto[1]([⊠])

[1] Universidade Tecnológica Federal do Paraná (UTFPR), Curitiba, Brazil
juan.barata.si@gmail.com, {bastos,adolfo}@utfpr.edu.br
[2] Universidade Federal do Pará (UFPA), Belém, Brazil
diegolisboa@ufpa.br

Abstract. Requirements Engineering (RE) is one of the prime areas in software development. Since agile software development englobes several emerging techniques and advocates for continuous improvement, it urges the question of which agile RE practices are currently most used, their characteristics, and the challenges in their employment. The aim of this work is to investigate and categorize the collection and specification of agile requirements practices based on how professionals perceive their importance for a software project that applies agile methodologies. Thus, a survey was carried out with forty-six (46) Brazilian software development professionals, inquiring which methods are used for the collection and specification of agile requirements, as well as the features, benefits, and difficulties when employing the methods. The responses allowed us to perform data analysis and identify the relationships between the respondents' experience and the viewpoints on the collection methods and the agile requirements specification. In addition, it was noted that the adoption of these methods is still very recent. They have mainly been used for less than five years. Moreover, it was noted that, for most respondents, there are yet significant challenges and advances to be made for better efficiency in applying the informed methods.

1 Introduction

The main objective of requirements engineering (RE) is to identify the demands of stakeholders, which are people or organizations that will be affected by the system and possess influence, direct or indirect, over the system requirements. Consequently, it is essential to understand the issue and its context, elicit the requirements for the system, analyze, document, and validate them [14].

RE is intended to elicit, organize, and document the software requirements based on a process that establishes and maintains an agreement among stakeholders [8]. It is a communication process that will stipulate what the software must do, its functions, essential and desirable properties, and restrictions [23].

RE practices employed by agile teams differ from those applied in traditional RE [5]. Similar to any process, RE must be continuously improved. Agile software development

C. Rocha et al. (Eds.): WBMA 2021, CCIS 1642, pp. 110–119, 2023.
https://doi.org/10.1007/978-3-031-25648-6_9

methods recommend adopting a step-by-step approach to improve software development processes and adaptation to the altered conditions (e.g., focusing on introducing or improving unique practices) rather than changing all at once.

Over the years, many survey studies conducted have investigated the selection level of agile practices [1, 2, 4, 6, 7, 9, 15, 17–19, 21] in software development projects, including the 'State of Agile' report (Digital.ai, 2020). Therefore, it is apparent the importance of agile methods and their practices for the software development industry.

The research question in this study is based on the following gap: "What are the main techniques, characteristics, and challenges of employing agile methods in the collection and specification of requirements?". We described the employment of the collection and specification of agile requirements adopted by software development companies, focusing on techniques, characteristics, and challenges of the technique practitioners. A survey was carried out, where forty-six (46) participants and practitioners from thirty-one (31) Brazilian companies (public and private) answered about the numerous collection and specification techniques of agile requirements. The results exhibited an overview of the employment of these techniques in private and public organizations.

The remainder of this work is organized as follows: Sect. 2 presents the description of the work reports; Sect. 3 displays the research methodology; Sect. 4 shows the research report; Sect. 5 presents the discussion and conclusion of the study.

2   State of the Art

Recently, the literature has described the employment of RE in projects that adopt agile methods and demonstrated their importance since one of the main reasons for software projects failures is the poor collection of requirements [11]. According to SAITO [20], a successful software project depends on the quality of the Software Requirements Specification (SRS) model. SRS inadequately done is a catalyst for other issues throughout the software project, mainly when the process adopts agile forms of software development, as many practitioners skip some steps and produce important artifacts, causing inefficiency in the requirements specification.

In the work published by MEDEIROS [16], the author emphasizes that an inadequate SRS is an enhancer of other issues throughout the software project, especially when applying agile methods. According to the author, it was indicated that in agile environments, SRS are generally superficial, insufficient, and inadequate. Consequently, the author proposed an agile approach for SRS, using a set of good practices from Agile-RE, such as Agile Modeling, Prototypes, and Scenario Testing features, in order to propose an agile SRS process.

Thus, by examining several techniques and approaches for the collection and specification of requirements in agile software development projects, this work aims to investigate the techniques, characteristics, and challenges in the collection and specification of agile requirements currently employed by private and public companies through a questionnaire, to collect accurate data on the full adoption of agile methods in software development.

3 Research Methodology

This study aims to illustrate the characteristics and challenges in employing the collection and specification of agile requirements by private and public companies. A survey was carried out as the research method. According to WOHLIN [25], surveys are used when a technique or tool has already occurred or before it was conducted.

The characteristics are described for which agile method is employed, how the respondents first learned about Agile-RE, level of knowledge, time of use, and benefits achieved after applying the method. The challenges were defined through hypothesis and determined according to the authors cited in Sect. 2. Overall, a total of five (5) hypotheses were established, which are listed below:

- H1. Low client availability is a relevant challenge;
- H2. Inadequate c between client and team is a relevant challenge;
- H3. The lack of transparency between client's needs and solutions is a relevant challenge;
- H4. Inefficient change control in requirements is a relevant challenge;
- H5. Insufficient documentation for implementation, maintenance, and/or training is a relevant challenge.

3.1 Survey Validation

Before sharing, the survey was validated with the research group: a professor from Universidade Tecnológica Federal do Paraná (UTFPR), a professor from Universidade Federal do Pará (UFPA), a part of the software development team from Coordenadoria de Tecnologia da Informação e Comunicação da Pró-Reitoria de Ensino de Graduação (COTIC/PROEG) da UFPA and a part of the software development team from a private company. The questions from the pilot survey were answered by the research group and, after that, the survey feedback was made.

3.2 Planning and Scheduling the Survey

The survey was conducted virtually through the Google Forms platform. The link for the survey was shared in five social media: LinkedIn, Facebook, Instagram, WhatsApp, and Telegram. The collected data was stored in the Zenodo online repository and is available in the Portuguese version.

3.3 Analyzing the Results

The responses were analyzed through frequency and percentages that were automatically generated by the Google Forms platform.

4   Results

A total of forty-six (46) responses were collected, in which forty-four (44) respondents informed that they work with collection and specification of requirements, and only two respondents do not work with requirements but are a part of a software development team. 69.6% of respondents work in private companies and 30.4% in public companies. 91.7% of respondents work in national companies and 8.3% in multinational companies, working in different positions, as shown in Fig. 1.

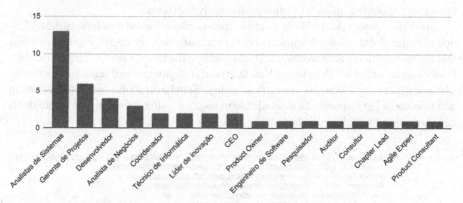

Fig. 1.   Distribution of working positions among the survey respondents.

4.1   Characterization of Employed Methods for the Collection of Requirements

In the first question of the questionnaire, we identified which methods are employed by companies for the collection of requirements by inquiring: "What is the main method used for the collection of requirements in software projects that employ agile methods?". Table 1 shows that Interviews with Stakeholders (56.6%), Lean Inception (17.4%), and Design Thinking (13%) are the most used methods.

Table 1.   Percentage of respondents that informed the use of each collection of requirements method.

Collection of requirements methods	Percentage of respondents (%)
Interview with stakeholders	56.6
Lean inception	17.4
Design thinking	13
Workshops	4.3
Lean Iron analysis	2.2
Others	2.2

114   J. C. Barata et al.

Based on the results, 4.4% of respondents stated that they learned about the method through internet research, 30.4% learned through the academy, 23.9% learned through training or courses, and 39.2% learned through their workplace.

As reported in the survey, 10.9% of respondents claimed that collection of requirements is used in their team for less than one (1) year, 23.9% use it between one (1) and two (2) years, 23.9% use it between two (2) and four (4) years, 8.7% use it between four (4) and five (5) years, and 32.6% use it for more than five (5) years. Moreover, 2.2% of respondents informed that they possess little knowledge about the method, 36.9% have intermediate knowledge, 28.3% have high knowledge, and 32.6% have enough knowledge about the method to consider themselves experts.

In the survey, we asked: "What would be the benefits achieved by adopting the collection of requirements methods employed in the company they operate?". Figure 2 exhibits that the main benefits achieved were: Understanding the client's needs, Scope visibility, Faster validation, MVP (Minimum Viable Product) alignment, and team collaboration. The least mentioned benefits were: Practicality, Standardization, and Satisfaction. In addition, three (3) respondents were unable to respond to the question. The respondents could mention more than one benefit.

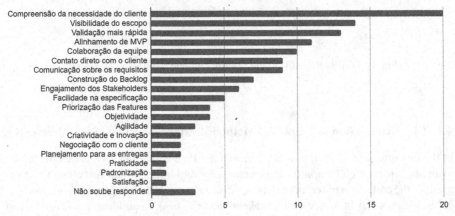

Fig. 2. Benefits of employing the collection of requirements methods mentioned by the respondents.

4.2 Characterization of Employed Methods for the Specification of Requirements

After finishing the questions about the collection of requirements, we seek to identify which methods are used for the specification of requirements. We asked: "What are the main methods employed for the specification of requirements in software projects that uses agile methods?". Table 2 displays the most used methods: Users History with 60.9%, Product Backlog Building (PBB) with 15.2%, and Prototypes with 13.0%.

Based on the results, 2.2% of respondents stated that they learned about the method through internet research, 21.8% learned through the academy, 41.3% learned through training or courses, and 34.8% learned through their workplace.

Table 2. Percentage of respondents that informed the use of each specification of requirements method.

Specification of requirements methods	Percentage of respondents (%)
Users history	60.9
Product Backlog Building (PBB)	15.2
Prototypes	13.0
Casos de uso	10.9

Concerning the time of use, 19.6% stated that specification of requirements is used in their team for less than one (1) year, 21.7% use it between one (1) and two (2) years, 32.6% use it between two (2) and four (4) years, 2.2% use it between four (4) and five (5) years, and 23.9% use it for more than five (5) years. Furthermore, 2.2% of respondents informed that they possess little knowledge about the method, 36.9% have intermediate knowledge, 32.6% have high knowledge, and 28.3% have enough knowledge about the method to consider themselves experts.

We also asked: "What would be the benefits achieved by adopting the specification of requirements methods employed in the company they operate?". Figure 3 reveals that the main benefits cited were: Clarity, Problem identification, Objectivity, Features Partitioning, and Features Listing. Adherence to the process, The use of documentation, and Standardization were the least mentioned benefits. The respondents could mention more than one benefit.

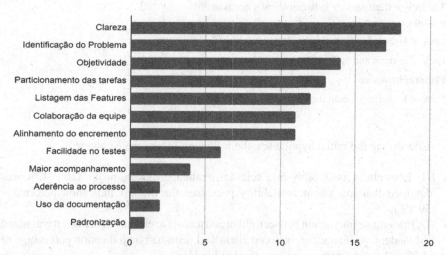

Fig. 3. Benefits of employing the specification of requirements methods mentioned by the respondents.

The questionnaire also included questions about the work team satisfaction with the employment of the collection and specification of requirements methods mentioned by the respondents. For 19.6% of respondents, the team is neither satisfied nor unsatisfied, 50% is more or less satisfied, and 30.4% is very satisfied.

4.3 Challenges in the Employment of the Collection and Specification of Requirements Methods

In order to verify and identify the challenges in the employment of the collection and specification of requirements methods, we asked: "What are the difficulties, limitations, challenges, and points to improve in the employment of the collection and specification of requirements methods?". 73.9% of respondents informed "Yes" and 26.1% informed "No". It is essential to highlight that the five (5) hypotheses of possible challenges were added to the question to verify their relevance. Table 3 shows the indication percentage that respondents marked as a challenge in employing the methods.

Table 3. Challenges in adopting the collection and specification of requirements mentioned by the respondents.

Challenges in adopting the collection and specification of requirements	Percentage of respondents (%)
Low client availability	39.5
Inefficient change control in requirements	18.4
Insufficient documentation	13.2
Inadequate interaction	13.2
The lack of transparency between client's needs and solution	5.3
Lack of knowledge from the development team	2.6
Lack of domain and agile mindset from the team	2.6
Platform limitations	2.6
Lack of knowledge about the methods	2.6

Concerning the initial hypotheses, the following results were obtained:

- H1. Low client availability is a relevant challenge: according to Table 4, it was identified that low client availability possesses the highest indication percentage (39.5%);
- H2. Inadequate interaction between client and team is a relevant challenge: it was noted that inadequate interaction between client and team had an indication percentage of 13.2%. The same percentage was observed in H5;
- H3. The lack of transparency between client's needs and solutions is a relevant challenge: it was observed that the lack of transparency between client's needs and solutions was the least indicated by respondents (5.3%);
- H4. Inefficient change control in requirements is a relevant challenge: H4 was the second most indicated challenge with a percentage of 18.4%;

- H5. Insufficient documentation for implementation, maintenance, and/or training is a relevant challenge: The percentage observed in H2 was the same as H5, with 13.2%.

5 Conclusions

This work aimed to describe the characteristics and challenges in employing the collection and specification of agile requirements by private and public companies. A survey was carried out as the research method, where forty-six (46) responses were collected from practitioners in software analysis and development teams. The results showed the characteristics and challenges of the collection and specification of requirements methods adopted by private and public companies when using agile software development methods.

In projects that employ agile methods, when analyzing the collection of requirements, it was observed that the main applied methods are Interviews with Stakeholders, Lean Inception, and Design Thinking. In addition, it was noticed that these methods are being used for less than five (5) years (67.4% of respondents). However, 32.6% of respondents stated that they know enough about the methods to consider themselves experts. The main benefits in using the collection of requirements methods mentioned by the respondents are: Understanding the client's needs, Scope visibility, and Faster validation.

In relation to the specification of requirements in projects that employ agile methods, the Users History, PBB, and Prototypes were the most mentioned methods used. It was also noticed that 73.9% of respondents use these requirements methods for less than four (4) years, and 97.8% consider themselves with intermediate, high, and advanced knowledge about the methods. According to the respondents, the main benefits in employing the specification of requirements methods are: Clarity, Problem identification, and Objectivity.

Concerning the challenges and points to improve in the employment of collection and specification of agile requirements, 73.9% of respondents informed that there are challenges and points of improvement. The four (4) main relevant challenges identified were: low client availability, inefficient change control in requirements, insufficient documentation for implementation, maintenance, and/or training is a relevant challenge, and inadequate interaction between client and team.

Therefore, the collected data suggest that the employment of collection and specification of agile requirements are still very recent and are mainly used for less than five (5) years, but there are several knowledgeable workers that can apply these methods accordingly. Nevertheless, for most respondents, the collection and specification of requirements still have significant challenges and improvements for their proper and efficient use.

Overall, the data allows new research options for the future, such as "what strategies could be applied to obtain more availability from clients?", "what can be done to maintain an efficient change control in requirements?", "how to maintain and improve the interaction with stakeholders?", and "how to improve projects documentation?". These research options can assist in improving the employment of Agile-RE in software analysis and development project teams in private and public organizations.

References

1. Ali, M.A.: Survey on the state of agile practices implementation in Pakistan. Int. J. Inf. Commun. Technol. Res. **2**(4) (2012)
2. Barabino, G., Grechi, D., Tigano, D., Corona, E., Concas, G.: Agile methodologies in web programming: a survey. In: Cantone, G., Marchesi, M. (eds.) XP 2014. LNBIP, vol. 179, pp. 234–241. Springer, Cham (2014). https://doi.org/10.1007/978-3-319-06862-6_16
3. Boness, K.D., Harrison, R., 2007. Goal sketching: towards ágil requirements engineering. In: second International Conference on Software Engineering Advances (ICSEA)
4. Buchalcevova, A.: Research of the Use of Agile Methologies in the Cezch Replubic. Springer, Information Systems Development (2009)
5. Cao, L., Ramesh, B.: Agile requirements engineering practices: an empirical study. Softw. IEEE **25**(1), 60–67 (2008)
6. Causevic, A., Sundmark, D., Punnekkat, S.: An industrial survey on contemporary aspects of software testing. In: Proceedings of 3rd International Conference on Software Testing, Verification and Validation (ICST). IEEE (2010)
7. Doyle, M., Williams, L., Cohn, M., Rubin, K.S.: Agile software development in practice. In: Cantone, G., Marchesi, M. (eds.) XP 2014. LNBIP, vol. 179, pp. 32–45. Springer, Cham (2014). https://doi.org/10.1007/978-3-319-06862-6_3
8. Engholm, H.: Engenharia de Software na Prática, Novatec, São Paulo (2010)
9. Hussain, Z., Slany, W., Holzinger, A.: Current state of agile user-centered design: a survey. In: Holzinger, A., Miesenberger, K. (eds.) USAB 2009. LNCS, vol. 5889, pp. 416–427. Springer, Heidelberg (2009). https://doi.org/10.1007/978-3-642-10308-7_30
10. Inayat, I., Salim, S.S., Marczak, S., Daneva, M., Shamshirband, S.: A systematic literature review on agile requirements engineering practices and challenges. Compt. Human Behav. **51**, 915–929 (2016)
11. Kassab, M.: The changing landscape of requirements engineering practices over the past decade. In: Proceedings of 5th International Workshop on Empirical Requirements Engineering (EmpiRE). IEEE (2015)
12. Kassab, M.: An empirical study on the requirements engineering practices for agile software development. In: Proceedings of 40th EUROMICRO Conference on Software Engineering and Advanced Applications (SEAA). IEEE (2014)
13. Kassab, M., Neill, C., Laplante, P.: State of practice in requirements engineering: contemporary data. Innov. Syst. Softw. Eng. **10**(4), 235–241 (2014). https://doi.org/10.1007/s11334-014-0232-4
14. Kotonya, G., Sommerville, I.: Requirements engineering with viewpoints. Softw. Eng. J. **11**, 5–18 (1998)
15. Kurapati, N., Manyam, V.S.C., Petersen, K.: Agile software development practice adoption survey. In: Wohlin, C. (ed.) XP 2012. LNBIP, vol. 111, pp. 16–30. Springer, Heidelberg (2012). https://doi.org/10.1007/978-3-642-30350-0_2
16. Medeiros, J.R.V.: Na approach to support the requirements specification in agile software development (2017)
17. Nazir, N., Hasteer, N., Bansal, A.: A survey on agile practices in the Indian it industry. In: Proceedings of 6th International Conference on Cloud System and Big Data Engineering (Confluence). IEEE (2016)
18. Papatheocharous, E., Andreou, A.S.: Empirical evidence and state of practice of software agile teams. J. Softw. **26**(9) (2014)
19. Rodríguez, P., Markkula, J., Oivo, M., Turula, K.: Survey on agile and lean usage in Finnish software industry. In: Proceedings of International Symposium on Empirical Software Engineering and Measurement (ESEM). ACM-IEEE (2012)

20. Saito, S., Takeuchi, M., Hiraoka, M., Kitani, T.: Requirements clinic: third party inspection methodology and practice for improving the quality of software requirements specifications. In: 21st IEEE International Requirements Engineering Conference (RE) (2013)

21. Salo, O., Abrahamsson, P.: Agile methods in European embedded software development organisations: a survey on the actual use and usefulness of extreme programming and scrum. IET Softw. 2(1), 58–64 (2008)

22. Solinski, A., Petersen, K.: Prioritizing agile benefits and limitations in relation to practice usage. Softw. Qual. J. 24(2), 447–482 (2014). https://doi.org/10.1007/s11219-014-9253-3

23. Sommerville, I.: Software Engineering, 7th edn., Addison Wesley, Boston (2018)

24. Wang, X., Zhao, L., Wang, Y., Sun, J.: The role of requirements engineering practices in agile development: an empirical study. In: Zowghi, D., Jin, Z. (eds.) requirements engineering. CCIS, vol. 432, pp. 195–209. Springer, Heidelberg (2014). https://doi.org/10.1007/978-3-662-43610-3_15

25. Wohlin, C., Runeson, P., Höst, M., Ohlsson, M.C., Regnell, B., Wesslén, A. Experimentation in Software Engineering. Springer, Berlin (2012). https://doi.org/10.1007/978-3-642-29044-2

Author Index

Printed in the United States
by Baker & Taylor Publisher Services